White Goats and Black Bees

White Goats and Black Bees

DONALD GRANT

Illustrations by JOHN MURRAY

Doubleday & Company, Inc., Garden City, New York, 1974

Library of Congress Cataloging in Publication Data
Grant, Donald, 1911–
    White goats and black bees.
    Personal reminiscences of life in rural Ireland.
    1. Farm life—Ireland—Cork (County)   I. Title.
S522.I73G7   914.19'5'039
ISBN 0-385-06522-1
Library of Congress Catalog Card Number 73–18776

To Jeremiah Daly

"Jeremiah smokes his pipe
and makes the clouds that hang
above the mountains."*

*From a poem written in Dooneen by Alissa Swerdloff of New York
City when she was sixteen years old.*

Contents

Notes and Acknowledgments 9

Of Roses and Decisions 15

Cork and Kerry 23

A Priest by the Roadside 33

Retirement 43

Communication Means People 53

Land Hunger 65

Gales, Lambs and a Kitten 75

Two Goats in Kid 85

Settling Down 95

Goats Are for Tinkers 105

Christmas Candles on the Mountain 117

A Ham in the Chimney 129

[7]

Contents

An American Peasant   *141*

Learning to Know Our Neighbors   *151*

Birth Is a Tender Struggle   *163*

Life Is for Confronting   *173*

Guests Are Welcome—Sometimes   *185*

An Irish Policeman—in Ireland   *197*

Lords and Ladies Are After Going   *207*

An Organic Whole   *219*

Animals Are for Friendship   *231*

Where Is Dooneen?   *243*

Of Milk and Honey   *255*

A Year Is Only a Beginning   *267*

Shades of Black   *279*

Some Problems Solve Themselves   *291*

Love, the Sea and the Mountains   *301*

Appendix   *313*

Notes and Acknowledgments

A perceptive friend who visited us in Dooneen expressed some admiration for the life we had developed here, but added to me: "You could never do this without Mary." It is true of our farming operations and perhaps even more true of the writing of this book. It is the story of a mutual experience; I cannot say which ideas are my wife's and which are mine.

Our Irish friends and neighbors have been vastly kind and patient in teaching us about rural Ireland. Of the approximately 1,200 people in our parish there are few, if any, to whom we are not in some way indebted.

The Reverend T. J. Walsh, who was parish priest when we arrived and later was transferred to Blackrock, Cork City, was from the beginning, and has continued to be, our chief guide not only concerning things Irish but in many other things temporal and spiritual, besides. He is not, however, responsible for the imperfections that may have crept into this book.

Equally innocent of my errors is Tadhg ODonnabhain, that most remarkable of Irish teachers and farmers, whose visits to Dooneen have been valuable seminars on Irish history and life.

Spelling Irish place-names has been a special hazard. They are translated into English phonetically; sounds reach different ears variously. I have chosen to render the name of our peninsula as Muintirvara although good authority can be found for several other forms. Father Walsh likes Muintirvara best and so, reportedly, does the Bishop of Cork. However spelled in English, its name was a part of the oral tradition of our peninsula even before the Celts arrived here. A leader of the pre-Celtic peoples was called Baire. Muintirvara means the people of Baire.

Many in the United States have helped us in our Irish adventure and in writing about it. For the last quarter of a century before we came to Ireland I was employed by the St. Louis *Post-Dispatch,* most of the time writing about foreign affairs. Joseph Pulitzer, Jr., the editor and publisher, and Evarts A. Graham, Jr., the managing editor, have been tolerant of my change of interests and venue. From Ireland I have written a column on country life for the *Post-Dispatch.*

I am especially grateful to the readers of that newspaper, many of whom have written us and some of whom have come to Dooneen to pay us a visit. I hope they will see this book as a reply to the letters which I did not have the time or energy to answer in the usual way.

This book would not have been possible without the help of Ken McCormick of Doubleday.

Nor, for that matter, would it have been possible for me to find time to write this book without the help of Jimmy Daly of Cahir, the next townland to the west of us, who helped

Notes and Acknowledgments

Mary from time to time with the animals and the garden while I worked at my typewriter.

Finally, I must acknowledge my great and eternal debt to the dogs Job and Prince; to the cat Padraic; to the goats Fleur, Katrina, Joy and Paddy; to our 200,000 black Irish bees; to the many wild birds, which continue to deserve the prayers of a St. Francis; and to all of the other non-human creatures of Dooneen, not excluding the many graceful foxes I have seen or the badgers who have eluded me, though I have found their traces. Each creature in its own way has taught me much. Some have given me love, besides; I return that, with deepest gratitude.

DONALD GRANT
*Dooneen, Kilcrohane,
Bantry, County Cork,
Ireland*

White Goats and Black Bees

Of Roses and Decisions

Mary and I walked away from our city penthouse and our well-paying jobs as newspaper and magazine correspondents writing about world affairs. We left behind a life of luxury and glamour, accepting a reduction in our income by something more than 80 per cent.

We began a new life as peasants on a rocky scrap of land in a remote corner of Ireland.

We knew nothing about farming, excepting what one might learn by growing roses on a terrace high above the city's noisome streets. Mary sold her automatic dishwasher to the tenant who took over our penthouse. I donated my white tie and tails to Peruvian Relief.

The great change began casually. One summer day Mary and I were seated on our terrace, in the shade of the awning, I with my Agatha Christie and Mary with her seed catalogue. The steady splash of the fountains made a pleasant sound against the background blare of taxi horns.

"You know," I said, looking up from my book, "farming has

always appealed to me. Since I was a kid I have always wanted to be a farmer."

It was a distinctly odd thing to have said. My entire life had been spent in cities—as, for that matter, had Mary's.

She didn't look up from her seed catalogue, and only mumbled something about sweet peas. Then my statement registered and she did look up.

"So have I," she said, crisply, "so why don't we?"

"So why don't we what?" I asked vapidly, not having taken my own suggestion seriously.

"Become farmers."

I put my book aside. I could think of several reasons why my suggestion, and Mary's response to it, were at least light-hearted if not light-minded. We had no farm, little money to buy one and no spare time to work at farming while we learned what it was all about. Our jobs were demanding—and rewarding. Physically we were hardly up to the tasks farming entailed. We were not young. We had spent too much time reading, writing and talking—while sitting down.

"Go ahead and read," said Mary. "I won't be a minute."

An hour later Mary returned to the terrace. Meanwhile she had canvassed the farm-for-sale advertisements in several newspapers and magazines and had put in a few telephone calls. That was the beginning: one step led to another.

While I had continued reading on the terrace Mary's efforts had washed out California and Florida—too expensive, too many old people. Subsequent researches of locations elsewhere on the North American continent also led up blind alleys. It seemed to be a crowded place; land values were high. We both liked New England, but the winters were impossibly cold.

The search revealed one thing: we knew what we wanted.

Both of us had been born inland. We wanted to live on the ocean, but within sight of mountains. We wanted a good climate for growing things and one that was reasonably comfortable for ourselves.

Mary's work, and mine, had involved people of various cultures. Mary had worked in India, in the Middle East and in Latin America. My specialty was Asia, Africa and Latin America. Aside from our travels we had spent a good deal of time at the United Nations, using its resources in following moves on the international chessboard. We had, therefore, already discovered that the world was full of people, some of them quite pleasant, who did not happen to be Americans.

On the other hand, picking a spot in which to build a new life was different from visiting a place as a traveling journalist. Cultural change could be a happy challenge—if it were a challenge we could meet. Neither of us was very good at languages.

Southern Italy, for instance, appealed to me a great deal. Both of us were fond of Greece, particularly the Greek islands, and we liked the Greek people. We did not fancy Greek politics. Italians, and Greeks, insisted on speaking their own languages and we neither spoke these languages nor were likely to learn to do so with any great proficiency.

Area by area we considered every part of the globe as a possible site for our new home. We had vacationed in the West Indies and the experience had been a happy one. To live there without a yacht, however, would be déclassé. A yacht was one of the many things we couldn't afford.

It was sobering to consider our financial situation.

If you considered our annual income we were prosperous enough. A glamorous city life is an expensive way of living.

What we earned we spent. Still, we could contemplate economies and various means for scraping the barrel. Our plan was to buy a small rural place and to reconstruct it to our taste out of income as much as possible. We could use it for holidays, at first, and do much of the work on it ourselves. Later would be time enough to consider uprooting ourselves altogether.

We were walking together from our Manhattan apartment to the United Nations one day when I said the magic word: "Ireland."

That stopped Mary in her tracks. "You're mad," she said.

Neither of us had any meaningful family tradition of Irish origins. Both of our families had been American for many generations. We were Protestants; Ireland was a Catholic country. Ireland was one of the few places on earth that neither Mary nor I had visited.

We had known a few Irish diplomats at the United Nations. Mary had a young Irish friend in the United Nations secretariat, a girl who had returned to Ireland to be married.

"You and Donald must come and visit us," she said as Mary saw her off.

"But why on earth would we be coming to Ireland?" was Mary's response.

Mary had been thinking in terms of world politics. Ireland was not a great power.

The Irish girl only smiled.

Mary recalled this conversation when I suggested Ireland as a future home.

"But the fact is," I replied, relying on nothing more solid than a general idea of geography, "that Ireland has mountains;

it is an island, so the sea surrounds it. The culture is different enough to be interesting—but the Irish do speak English.

"Ireland, also, is a developing country—richer than Asia, Africa or Latin America, but poor by North American or even by European standards. Maybe we could find a place we could afford. Ireland has a relatively thin population; there must be a few wild places left, not far from mountains and the sea."

When we returned to the apartment that night Mary started rummaging through old piles of papers in the back of a closet.

"Gordon," she explained. While I was trying to figure that out, Mary surfaced.

Before we were married, she reminded me, she had once had a small apartment on First Avenue, just facing the United Nations. It was there that she had given vent to her first impulse toward rural living, by growing roses in wooden tubs on the fire escape. Her landlord had objected to the roses, which was a pity, for Mary had achieved a balanced ecology of sorts. Whenever there were street demonstrations in front of the United Nations, which was fairly often, the mounted police would rush to the scene to control the crowds.

Their horses left droppings behind them. When the shouting was over, Mary would collect the droppings to fertilize her roses.

If the roses must go, Mary told the landlord, she would go with them. So she did, and when she sublet the apartment it was to a thin man with a bald head, who smoked a long-stemmed pipe. Because she liked his ironic smile Mary let the new tenant have her air conditioner, some paintings and a few pieces of furniture. It began a friendship.

The new tenant was an Irishman named Gordon Clark. At the time he was employed by the Irish Tourist Board on a New York assignment. When his job there was done and he returned to Dublin he gave Mary a number of books and pamphlets about Ireland. It was this material that Mary now was recovering from among a pile of old papers in the closet. Neither Mary nor I had read the books and pamphlets about Ireland. We read them now.

I also talked to Frank Aiken, the Irish Foreign Minister, who frequently visited the United Nations. I had always liked Aiken. We had a good talk about a number of things, including the possibility of my building a new life, with Mary, in rural Ireland.

"It will be a change," he said with a wise twinkle. He meant that it would be a change not only from our life in New York City but that rural Ireland would lead us to a different kind of life than one might find in any city—Milwaukee, Minneapolis, London, Paris or Rome.

Meanwhile, Mary wrote a letter to Gordon Clark, in Dublin. He found the idea of our settling in Ireland amusing.

"You'd better make a trip to Ireland to see it for yourselves before making up your mind," Gordon wrote back. So we booked a passage on Aer Lingus.

I bought a copy of Frank O'Connor's *A Short History of Irish Literature* at Kennedy Airport. Mary slept on the plane, as she usually managed to do.

More than once on that journey I looked up from my book and wondered why we had come. Why buy a farm at all, and with what, and why in Ireland? Doubts. We could not hope to operate a farm ourselves for many years. Retirement was nearly a decade away and I might want to stay on even longer.

Even to spend holidays on an Irish farm might prove complicated. Meanwhile journalism absorbed most of my energies; taking on another interest seemed almost a species of disloyalty.

Gordon Clark met us at Shannon Airport, bringing the two youngest of his children with him. He just happened to be in the neighborhood, he said, while showing the children that part of Ireland. Of course we did not believe him. It was typically generous of Gordon to meet us like that. We joined Gordon and the children for two days of motoring about Counties Clare and Limerick.

The sunlight was filtered, the shadows soft. There seemed to be an endless series of towers, with rooks flying; of small, whitewashed stone cottages with thatched roofs and with peat smoke coming from the chimneys; of green fields and sparkling streams—and of happy children, pink-faced and blue-eyed.

The scene did tricks with time, for me. It all seemed to belong to the world I had known as a child, when I would take long walks with my grandfather. I was fond of my grandfather.

Wherever we went, on that first exploration of Ireland, we seemed to encounter good manners. Teas and dinners invariably were at little places where our host or hostess seemed happy we had come; they smiled, and served good food graciously. We tasted Irish soda bread for the first time and liked it. Once we had dinner in a castle, where harps were played and songs sung while we sipped mead from pottery bowls.

One might almost suspect Gordon Clark of arranging it all —Potemkin village after Potemkin village—though of course that was not possible, even for an Irishman. There must be something real behind the pleasant facade.

Before Gordon left us, the idea of making a new home in Ireland seemed considerably less absurd. A vague possibility had become a dream and the dream was becoming great with fulfillment.

Quietly, before he went his way, Gordon asked if we had settled on any particular part of Ireland where we might wish to look at farms. Mary and I had, in fact, decided to look first in Kerry and then in Cork, though this was the first time the question had arisen in Gordon's presence. We told him, now.

With no change of expression, Gordon handed us a piece of paper. On it were lists of his friends who might help us in a search for an Irish farm. Half of the names on the list were of people in Kerry, half in West Cork.

It was a gesture with a touch of sorcery in it; the magic of Ireland was beginning.

Cork and Kerry

Alone in a rented car, Mary and I drove to Killarney, where we stood by a lake, listening to the evening song of birds. We watched swans floating off the shore as if they were reflections of the clouds which hung over the mountain across the lake. We slept there. In the morning we were surprised that it was all real.

Along Dingle Bay we went for a walk and were drawn by a small cottage because of the lush crop of flowers growing out of a thatched roof: daisies and foxglove. Fuchsia smothered a part of the cottage altogether.

Nearby the cottage a trout stream tumbled down the rocks. There were some green fields and a peat bog. There was a view of Dingle Bay.

We telephoned Dublin to thank Gordon for helping us and told him we had found the farm we had been looking for. He agreed it was wonderful but suggested mildly that before signing any papers we might just take a look at West Cork.

"Mind you," Gordon added, "many people have found

Kerry a pure delight." He paused. "But of course a few have gone mad there and there have been some murders . . ."

Like all Irishmen, we concluded, Gordon after all was a man of prejudice and absurd imagination. We saw no reason at all to delay purchase of the Dingle Bay paradise.

There were, as it turned out, a few complications.

A farmer and his mother had lived on the farm we wanted. When the mother died the farmer began drinking heavily. His brother, who lived and farmed nearby, tried to buy the home place but was turned down with an insult. The feud between the brothers seemed about to end in murder when the alcoholic brother packed a bag and left. Gone to England, the neighbors said. He could, presumably, be traced.

Neighbors advised us to avoid being seen by the brother who lived nearby and who had wanted to buy the farm. His lethal impulses, they thought, might be deflected to us, as prospective buyers.

Of course Mary and I did not take this story too seriously. The first step was to find the owner of the thatched cottage with foxglove growing from the roof. While the search was on we might as well be on our way.

We drove around the Ring of Kerry, saw the famous palm trees at Parknasilla, visited the beautiful gardens on Garinish Island in Bantry Bay, then pulled up at the Eldon Hotel in a place called Skibbereen, famous chiefly because so many people starved to death in the gutters there during the famine. The list of names Gordon had given us included that of a Skibbereen solicitor who might know of farms for sale. We reached him on the telephone and he came over for a visit with ourselves and Denis Murnane, also Gordon's friend and our host at the Eldon.

It was the sort of evening where no one mentions the purpose of it in the beginning because it wouldn't be polite and later, as—to use the phrase that seems always to crop up in newspaper reports of criminal trials in Ireland—drink was taken, no one could remember the purpose. Anyway it didn't happen that way to us. We had found our farm.

The next morning we put in a telephone call to Dingle. Still no word of the owner of the Kerry cottage.

Late that afternoon we strolled over to the office of the Skibbereen solicitor whom we had met the previous evening. We paused a moment to admire the dust and clutter of the outer room but as no one was there we pushed on into the solicitor's private office. There he was, leaned back in his chair, his feet on the desk, sound asleep.

We tried to leave quietly but he awoke. After a few minutes of vague muttering he shuffled the papers on his desk and came up with the list of West Cork properties he had forgotten to give us at the Eldon. He then excused himself with pleas of urgent business.

"A solicitor in a place like this," he said, "works like a slave." He looked at us with suffering eyes. We left.

Just to be able to tell Gordon that we had looked in West Cork we decided to follow up a few of the places on the list. Driving through the West Cork countryside was pleasant enough in any case.

There was a Georgian Mansion at Union Hall which might have been made habitable for around $20,000. It was interesting to see what a few years of rain, dripping through a leaking roof, will do to an upholstered couch. In front of the Georgian Mansion, though, was a really splendid monkey puzzle tree.

We turned to regions more remote, enjoying the scenery. The solicitor had crossed out one place on his list with the notation: "Not suitable. Back of the beyond." Intrigued by the phrase, we decided to take a look. It wasn't easy to find. We made several inquiries along the way and were directed wrongly with great confidence.

Ultimately we did find what seemed to be the house located in a wasteland of rocks, heather and furze, with the Atlantic at our feet. We parked the car and walked around. We were just getting back into the automobile when a woman hailed us in a hearty English voice. So glad we had come. She would show us the house.

Mary didn't much like it. Worms, she said later; you could feel them crawling in the woodwork. The kitchen was impossible. There were two small bathrooms downstairs and none up. For those needing such facilities in the middle of the night there was a very steep stairway, a booby trap.

Still, there was a lovely gadget in the living room fireplace. When you turned a wheel a blower fanned the fire. We praised it.

Back in Skibbereen Lil Murnane, Denis's wife, assured us that no one, but no one could exist in so remote and wild a spot. Anyway the Englishwoman had wanted something like $15,000 for the place—nothing extra for the worms but still a great deal more money than we had or could get hold of. Already we had checked out the possibility of a mortgage, with small payments over the years. It didn't exist for foreigners. No hope. Mary got out a road map to find the best way back to Dingle.

That night I dreamed I was back in New York on our

sunny apartment terrace. Only the sun suddenly was too bright. I opened my eyes to see that Mary had turned on the light and was dressing.

I looked at my watch. It was 7 A.M.

"Mary," I said, "you are walking in your sleep."

The idea of Mary being awake at that hour hadn't occurred to me. She is the world's best sleeper, bar none. Once she slept through a major riot, undisturbed.

"I've been thinking," she said. "About that place we saw yesterday . . ."

"The one with the monkey puzzle tree?"

"No, idiot, the place the Englishwoman showed us."

I was awake now. As Mary pulled on her third sweater I repeated with increasing emphasis that there was no possibility, but none at all, that we could buy that house or could live in it if we did buy it. Not even for vacations. Not even . . .

"I know," said Mary, "but anyway I want to see it again."

"At this hour?"

"As good as any," she said. "I can't sleep, thinking about it."

Argument was useless. We crept out of the hotel. No living thing was in sight. Early rising is not a West Cork virtue.

At a town named Durrus I thought I saw smoke coming from a chimney and pounded on a pub door. In nightgown and slippers the landlord's wife greeted us and agreed to cook breakfast, with something less than full Irish enthusiasm. We ate in a silence that was punctuated by snores coming from a relic of the night before, a man asleep on a bench in the pub.

We did learn that the body of water we would follow west from there to our destination was called Dunmanus Bay. The road was narrow and winding, following the margin of the bay. When we arrived Mary took little notice of the house. We walked on down the lane, between hedges, to the sea.

Blackbirds, thrushes and robins sang mightily. Pink light streaked the sky. Mountains appeared out of the mist across the bay and the fog rolled up to reveal green pastures on the mountainside behind us. Furze bushes were golden carpets leading to the water's edge. The open Atlantic was just ahead. A cock crowed, a donkey brayed. It was morning and all was right with the world. When it was time to leave Mary wept, her tears mingling with a light rain that had begun to fall.

We nearly missed seeing a young man walking along the road in our direction. I stopped to give him a lift. We weren't in a conversational mood but the young man was trying to be pleasant.

"Looking at that house for sale back there?" he asked.

No, I replied. We didn't have that kind of money.

"If it's a house ye'd be wanting," the young man continued, "my father has one he'll sell ye for fifteen hundred pounds."

We took our passenger to the village of Kilcrohane and let him out, then turned around and went back. Ten minutes later we had agreed to buy the house for 1,500 pounds— about $3,750.

Bargaining over the price was something we quickly saw would be useless with the young man's father, Jeremiah Daly. Once we had agreed to buy the place and he to sell it we were equally sure that the work of the solicitors would be a mere formality. Jeremiah Daly could be depended on.

He made no attempt to disguise the fact that a great deal needed to be done to the house. It had not been lived in for thirty years, he said. He had used the second floor for storing grain—which meant that the roof was tight, though he didn't say that. Old harness, barrels of salt herring and a few potatoes were stored on the ground floor. Worms had got into the wood, he said. Doors drooped by one corner.

The house was tucked back from the lane, all but hidden by hedges. To Mary and me it cried to be put in repair, to be lived in, cherished.

Pushing our way through the debris we could see that there had been six small rooms with a fireplace in each. The house was a plain box, built of stone and clay two or three hundred years ago. At some time it had been smeared with mortar inside and out, but the mortar was crumbling now. It had a slate roof and three chimney masses. At either end of the roof were chimney pots with small hearts cast in the terra cotta.

Surrounding the haggard were four stone outbuildings grouped about a manure pile. Centuries of muck caked the inside of the outbuildings. The house itself was built into a slope, a part of the land, as Frank Lloyd Wright used to say a house should be. Surrounding the house, and going with it, was about an acre of land broken by hedges well planted with olearia, fuchsia and escallonia, some with pollarded trees as well.

The house was in an area known as Dooneen. Why it was called that took a little sorting out. Dooneen, we learned, meant little fort in Irish. After some questioning we were shown a small grove of pine trees close by a cliff overhanging the bay. We walked there and discovered that there were two wide, circular ditches, now heavily overgrown. Standing in this ring fort, constructed three thousand years ago, one had a clear view of the bay, the rocky shore, and the open Atlantic.

Dunmanus Bay was named after a castle which had belonged to the O'Mahony clan. From our house you could see the castle, across the bay.

Dooneen, named after the ring fort, was a townland. The term townland puzzled us for a time. There were only three houses in Dooneen. Later we learned that before the great famine in the middle of the nineteenth century there had been some fifteen houses in Dooneen. The surrounding land was considered as being attached to the town and was farmed largely by co-operative effort, a communal enterprise. The same pattern existed all over West Cork and beyond. The townland became a term to designate the smallest division of a parish.

Dooneen was located toward the end of a peninsula jutting into the Atlantic off the southwest coast of Ireland, an arrow aimed more or less at New York. The peninsula was named Muintirvara, a name that was a part of the oral tradition here even before the Celts arrived. The parish, also named Muintirvara, extends inland a bit from the peninsula and is twenty-four miles long and about four miles wide. Parish records show that most of the 350 families in the parish have lived in roughly the same location for at least 700 years. Relationships between the O'Mahonys, the Dalys, the McCarthys, the O'Donovans and the rest have remained about the same during that time.

It was apparent from the outset that for Mary and me to live in Dooneen would be like a couple of Hottentots moving into Buckingham Palace. Americans, accustomed to Irish immigrant neighbors in the United States, often are surprised by the cultural differences between themselves and the rural Irish on their home ground. We were beginning to see some of those differences but we were determined to fit in if we could and were eager to begin.

We never did hear from the owner of that Kerry cottage, our first love.

A Priest by the Roadside

Having agreed with Jeremiah Daly to buy the place in Dooneen we felt it was ours and considered moving out of the Eldon Hotel immediately, taking sleeping bags to our new home. It was of course an absurd notion. Our home was in New York, in that apartment with fountains playing on the terrace. The house in Dooneen lacked all of what any middle-class American would consider the essentials—water piped in, a bathroom, electricity, cooking facilities, central heating. We weren't even sure the fireplaces would work and in any event we had no fuel.

Resisting that first impulse, therefore, we concentrated on making arrangements for having the place renovated so that we could stay there for our next vacation. We found a builder in Skibbereen and an architect. We learned all of the little by-road shortcuts between Skibbereen and Dooneen and drove back and forth frequently.

One thing that Gordon Clark had been most firm about was that we should make no final decision about buying a place until we had consulted Liam Collins. In fact we already had made such a decision, but when we telephoned Gordon to tell him that we had settled on West Cork rather than Kerry after all he seemed relieved but repeated his advice that we go talk to Liam. We did.

Collins, a nephew of Michael Collins, who perhaps more than any other single man was responsible for achieving Irish independence, was a solicitor in the town of Clonakilty. To see Liam Collins one waits in a small back room, on a broken chair, listening to the gossip of fellow litigants, interesting enough.

When it was our turn to see Collins he turned out to be a small man with jet black hair standing stiffly upright on his head. His eyes were very fierce but he had a perpetually amused smile. Before we got down to our problem naturally we talked a good bit about our mutual friend, Gordon Clark, and about the contrast in climatic conditions between the United States and Ireland.

Finally Collins began asking questions, making notes on slips of paper as we answered. We had agreed to buy some property? We were American citizens? Did we have any Irish relations? No? A pity. Purchasing Irish farmland might have been easier. Before we left he put the slips of paper, containing his notes, in a very large cardboard folder.

As a chatty afterthought Mary mentioned that we had found a contractor in Skibbereen who had agreed to fix up the house we had bought. There was a period of silence as Collins peered over his spectacles. He asked the name of the contractor. There was another pause.

"I'll be wanting to draw up a contract," said Collins. "A

very careful contract. You write out what you want done. Let me have it as soon as you can."

Mary suggested that no contract would in fact be needed, but Collins would hear none of it. "Your man can do good work, I can tell you," he said, "but bears watching. Yes, well, bears watching . . ."

Driving back to Skibbereen Mary fumed at Collins' suspiciousness and mistrust of that nice contractor. He was such a kindly and helpful man, the contractor was, a man of many interests. He ran a pub, made coffins and sometimes helped his friends with a bit of carpentry. Back at the Eldon, Denis Murnane's wife, Lil, laughed merrily when we told her the story. There had been some lawsuit involving the contractor, she said, but then you know how the Irish are, always going to court. Not to worry . . .

We talked it over with Jeremiah Daly. We might have done better, he said gently, if we had contracted with Anthony McCarthy, a neighbor from the next townland who had learned a bit of carpentry. We put this down as loyalty to the neighborhood. Skibbereen, after all, was in another parish.

So we returned to New York. On the way we stopped in Dublin to see some friends there. None had heard of Muintirvara peninsula—except Gordon. He smiled, puffed his pipe, and asked what it was the Irish Foreign Minister had told me about getting a house in Ireland. Something about it being a change, wasn't it? Well, Frank Aiken has not always been wrong, you know, said Gordon.

We were reminded of that as the taxi took us from Kennedy Airport, through Queens, to our Manhattan apartment. It was a hot, noisy journey. From the taxi we could see nothing but garish billboards and crowded housing, belching factory chimneys and scurrying people. Dooneen was different.

The following two years we commuted between New York and Ireland. In New York we were journalists as usual. In Ireland we were homesteaders, to use the phrase later suggested by Msgr. Luigi Ligutti of the Vatican, an expert on such matters.

Our first return to Dooneen was nearly a year after we had bought the house. After that we made two trips a year, returning for winter holidays as well as in summer. How we managed this with our respective employers I am still not quite sure. In all, I believe we made five trips to Ireland before we finally came to stay.

During the long months that elapsed between our purchase of the property in Dooneen and our first return we followed the progress of the builder, getting the house ready for our occupancy, as closely as we could from such a distance. Unfortunately the architect was overcome by a series of personal troubles and landed in the hospital; he was not much use to us. Lil Murnane and Kathleen Daly, Jeremiah's wife, were extremely helpful in correspondence. Lil kindly made several trips to Dooneen from Skibbereen and reported to us by mail. We also made a number of long-distance telephone calls to Ireland, which did nothing to ease our strained budget.

On our first return to Dooneen we rented a car at Shannon Airport and in our eagerness attempted to reach Dooneen by a shortcut through the mountains. We became hopelessly lost in a fog and it was so late and we were so tired after we finally found our way that we stopped at Skibbereen and bedded down at the Eldon. This was a pity because the Dalys, expecting us, had stayed up until 1 A.M. to be on hand for a proper welcome.

When we finally got to Dooneen the next morning we had a few surprises. Nothing had been heard of the trunk of household goods, including blankets, which we had dispatched from New York three months before our departure.

For central heating we had arranged to have electric storage heaters installed in the house. They were in place all right, put there by the government-owned Electricity Supply Board, which had, however, neglected to supply the current. The heaters work on a separate meter, turning on at night during the hours when the general demand for electricity is low and giving off their heat by day. They were quite cold.

It was indeed a cold day though summer by the calendar. Furthermore, the builder had left the windows open—and painted them that way. The house was frigid; we had no blankets for our bed and no heat.

The house itself was an island surrounded by rubble left by the builder. He also had neglected to provide for drainage around the house, as Jeremiah pointed out. There was nothing to prevent the rains from flowing in—and it does rain in Ireland.

Perhaps the greatest disappointment was in the floors. We had specified flagstones. What we got were small, thin pieces of broken shale, inadequately cemented in place. The first time we walked across the floor the stones began kicking loose.

Eventually, to be sure, everything did get straightened out. The first thing we did was get into our car and drive back to Skibbereen. There we bought blankets—and telephoned Liam Collins. Thank God for Liam Collins.

Armed with the contract, Collins made the builder remove the rubble, fix the drainage and replace the broken stones on the floor with slate. It all cost us a bit more but we came out of it with a fine house—and even tolerably good relations with the builder.

The Electricity Supply Board was difficult enough but in the course of time the storage heaters were connected. Meanwhile we had the fireplaces. The builder had done a good job there. Anyway the weather had turned warmer.

In retrospect the five trips to Dooneen before we moved there all seem to blend. There were many problems to be solved, much brutal physical labor to be done. We moved rocks, built flower beds, planted trees and shrubs by the dozen. We ached with fatigue, then grew numb.

Jeremiah's farmer son, Jerry, helped a great deal. He removed an old hay shed and a good stone barn that blocked our view of the sea and enclosed the haggard too tightly. Anthony McCarthy, the local builder Jeremiah had recommended to us in the first place, came around and renovated the three remaining stone barns. Gradually, as Mary and I traveled back and forth between New York and Dooneen, our Irish home took shape.

To save money for more important things we gave up the rented car and bought inexpensive motorbikes in Bantry. When we went to collect them at James O'Mahony's shop, we asked him how they ran.

"Like a bomb," he replied. He was right.

Mary was thrown by hers on our first try. She picked herself up in the center of Wolfe Tone Square, bruised but not seriously injured. We both had a bit more respect for the little machines after that.

As commuters we began to learn something about Ireland. You would stand beneath a cloudless sky, heart rejoicing at the poetry of it all, only to be pelted by hail and all but blown away by the wind a few minutes later. You could curse the brambles tearing at your clothes and skin and be soothed immediately by the taste of the blackberries between the thorns.

Back in New York we remembered Ireland, talked about Ireland, dreamed of our return.

One evening Mary and I were entertaining a small group of diplomats and their wives in our New York apartment when the telephone rang. Mary answered it and was told that McCarthy of the White House wished a word with her. It was flattering to have the Irish Mafia call from Washington, she thought, but the caller became more specific.

"You remember," he said, identifying himself, "McCarthy of the White House, the pub near Dooneen . . ."

Michael McCarthy, to be sure, had named his pub the White House. There are no pubs farther out on Muintirvara peninsula. As Michael often said, "The next Irish pub is in Boston."

The McCarthys were visiting relations in the United States. They came to dinner the next evening. For several hours, talking to the McCarthys, we forgot we were in New York; we might have been in Michael's pub, just up the road from Dooneen.

More and more, as we kept moving back and forth between America and Ireland we found ourselves spending leisure time in New York with Irish friends—diplomats, members of various Irish trade missions, students. I don't think our work as journalists suffered but increasingly, while in New York, we tended to look forward to our next trip to Ireland.

It was more than that. What we really were looking forward to was the time when we could be full-time homesteaders in Ireland.

When we began our series of visits to Ireland we were, I think, excessively aware that we were Protestants in a Catholic country. My father had once been a Methodist minister. Mary had been an Episcopalian Sunday School teacher, later a student of theology. We had heard all of the usual stories about Ireland as a priest-ridden place of strict censorship and bigotry. We were prepared for the worst.

On our first trip to Ireland after buying the place in Dooneen we rode our motorbikes one day to Durrus, a dozen miles away, to see Paddy O'Donovan, the blacksmith, about making a grill and some tongs for the fireplaces. He was at work at the forge; beyond the sparks was darkness.

When he finished with the piece of iron he was bending Paddy turned to us and we explained our errand. He agreed to make the things we wanted. As we turned to go we noticed the figure of another man in the gloom beyond the forge.

"Oh," said Paddy, "this is Father Walsh, the parish priest." He pronounced the name "Welsh" in the West Cork way. A brief but pleasant conversation followed. We liked the fact that Father Walsh had chosen to come for a chat with Paddy O'Donovan at his forge.

The nearest Protestant church also was in Durrus, a long motorbike ride away on a wet day. Our first Sunday in Dooneen we made it. Fortunately the sun shone, sparkling on the bay.

Going home, Mary, as usual, rode her bike on ahead and I followed on mine. Suddenly my motorbike coughed, then the motor stopped altogether and the bike glided to a halt. Not realizing what had happened Mary rode on and was soon out of sight. I pulled my bike off the road, sat on the seawall and lit my pipe; it was the only thing I could think to do.

A car stopped with one of our neighbors in it. We stuck our fingers in the motorbike petrol tank and they came out dry. The neighbor offered to bring me a can of petrol from Durrus.

The next car that stopped contained a middle-aged man dressed in black whom I recognized in a moment as the parish priest. He joined me on the wall and lit a pipe of his own. Then Mary came speeding back and soon the three of us were there in the sun.

For no good reason I explained that we were returning from services at the Protestant church in Durrus when my bike ran out of petrol.

"What a long way to go on a motorbike," he said, "just to attend church. Why don't you stop at your own village, Kilcrohane, at the Star of the Sea there?"

A little awkwardly I explained that both of us were lifelong Protestants.

"What harm? It's a free country," said Father Walsh. "You'd be welcome at the Star of the Sea I'm sure."

When we had got over that one Father Walsh started talking about Irish songs and to show what he meant he began singing some. By the time our neighbor came with the petrol we were all three singing together, sitting there on the seawall.

Retirement

⚰ The step from owning a "vacation home" where it might be fun to retire some day to actually retiring is a long one.

Such a step is the one just across Dunmanus Bay from Dooneen, at Canty's Cove. Years ago Mr. Canty had an inn of sorts there. It was popular with strangers, who were attracted by the pretty daughter of the house. Invariably the lodger was robbed during the night. When he complained the next morning he was invited to step out the back door. There was only one step there and in taking it the lodger dropped down the cliff and into the sea, which, incidentally, ended the complaints.

The shock of retirement is considerable for most men. It means the end of something that has taken up most of a man's waking thoughts and no little of his dream life for his adult existence. The whole meaning of things tends to be built around the job, even if to an outsider that job does not seem to be a particularly interesting one.

Being a stockbroker seems dull enough to me but one man

we knew blew out his brains rather than face retirement from a New York brokerage firm. I had seen many of my older newspaper colleagues resist retirement. The newspaper sometimes allowed an editor or writer to stay on beyond the age of sixty-five on a year-to-year basis. I had watched men suffer in this limbo. Some never lived to retire; I often wondered if the strain of uncertainty did not hasten the end.

Retiring before the age of sixty-five, on the other hand, carried severe penalties under the newspaper's pension plan. In addition I had heavy financial commitments which would not cease with retirement and Mary could expect no pension at all. When we retired, therefore, our income would be less than one fifth of the income to which we had been accustomed.

I was still in my fifties, in good health and enjoying my work as a newspaper correspondent writing about foreign affairs from the United Nations and on trips abroad. The idea was to quit while we were ahead.

I had been a newspaper writer and editor for forty years, which seemed long enough. I couldn't say I had saved the world—in most ways the world had become a less happy place for most people to live in, especially in the big cities. There was, perhaps, more hope for the millions in Asia, Africa and Latin America—but also more frustration. In any event I had seen enough of wars, revolutions and the general alienation of man from man.

The decision to retire to Ireland was Mary's as well as mine. We thought we could build a life there that was superior to the life we had known in New York in every way that was important. It was a challenge, to be sure. To meet it would take all of the health and vigor we still had—wasting assets by the nature of things. We could not see how delaying retirement to achieve a marginal increase in income would increase our chance for success.

I cannot pretend that I made the decision easily. I worry through problems. Mary, on the contrary, quit her job without a moment's hesitation. Her thing is faith. But then the Hagans, as Mary was born, were Irish once; she is an irrepressible optimist. The Grants were Scots, a gloomy people but stubborn.

We loaded our household goods on the *New Amsterdam,* one of the last of the gilded old Atlantic liners, and climbed aboard. For better or worse the umbilical cord was cut. It was a thoughtful journey.

When we neared the southwest coast of Ireland the world was shrouded in fog. Then, as the *New Amsterdam* approached Mizen Head Light, fog horn blasting, the fog momentarily cleared. From the deck we could see the little projection of land that was Dooneen, extending into Dunmanus Bay.

At Cobh we left the ship and huddled in the rain and made arrangements for our household goods to be sent on. Then we drove to Dooneen and slept.

We were awakened by birdsongs in August and got up to a world drenched in sunshine and life. Flowers bloomed everywhere. The hedges were fluttering with birds of every color and birdsongs filled the whole space between earth and sky.

We were in Ireland to stay. We looked out over the open Atlantic, to the west, and New York seemed far away. Surely it was no more than an early Irish legend, a place that never existed.

We knew then that we had come to Ireland because it is a beautiful place. Before I had ever visited Ireland I once had a

glimpse of it from the deck of a badly battered freighter, floundering in from the Atlantic crossing during World War II. Half of the convoy hadn't made it. It was midwinter but the Ireland I saw was a dream of spring, green fields running down to the sea.

The beauty was still there as Mary and I began to visit Ireland. As we visited again and again we discovered something more: Ireland was constructed on the human dimension. It was a small island. People there lived in small communities. They didn't pass each other by, they stopped and talked. In our part of Ireland, rural Ireland, you could wander any-where, day or night, and meet only friends. If you were hun-gry and thirsty and stopped at a strange cottage you would be given food and drink, a warm fire to sit by and a friendly bit of talk.

Life in rural Ireland was far more complete than in any city. Men and women related to each other in a more intimate way, and also with their farm animals and with nature. Just living was more exciting.

If living was to include eating, however, Mary and I some-how must contrive to produce most of the foodstuffs our-selves. Along every lane the brambles were laden with ripe berries—but man does not live by blackberries alone. An acre of ground, even an Irish acre—bigger than an American acre —is not very much land on which to feed a family, especially after subtracting space for a house and several stone barns, not to mention areas where there is nothing but rock.

The only good soil was in what we now call the orchard. During vacations we had planted there four apple trees and two plum trees—and scattered about elsewhere, three pear trees, two peach trees, three cherry trees and a fig tree. Our total crop to date consisted of half a dozen pears and two Cox's Orange Pippin apples. We also had a herb garden.

The plot containing the apple and plum trees was just east of the house. To keep weeds down we had spread large sheets of black plastic between the trees, held against the gales by an assortment of rocks and scrap lumber. We now proceeded to remove the plastic. There, in the orchard, we tilled the earth between the young trees and planted seeds we had brought with us.

August may not be the best month for planting but it was in

August that we came. A red-throated pipit, rare enough, followed us as we worked the soil. It was, we thought, a good omen.

As we planted Chinese cabbage, lettuce, carrots, mustard and kale we were distracted by the lovely meadows and hedges around us. They were in full color: purple loosestrife, scarlet pimpernel, meadow rue and blue sheep's-bit scabious all in bloom. Beyond our own east hedge was a fine pasture which we long had coveted. This three-acre tract of land, we thought, would go a long way toward helping us achieve self-sufficiency.

Meanwhile, a day or two after we had arrived in Dooneen our furniture caught up with us. The lorry driver managed to wedge his vehicle between two hedges just outside our gate, blocking the road completely.

A family of English tourists was trapped between the lorry and the sea. They had brought no food and the family included three hungry children. Mary invited them in to share what food we could find.

How long the lorry would have remained wedged in the lane is hard to say, if the lorry men had been left to their own devices. Nearly five hours after they had arrived at their predicament a group of students came along, headed for the seashore. Their little van was laden with skin-diving equipment. Tumbling out of the van they surveyed the situation, got to work and within a few minutes had the road cleared.

Meanwhile, the lorry men having lost interest in the household goods loaded on their vehicle, Mary and I had carried most of the things into our house. When, finally, we were left alone, we decided to sit down for a cup of tea at the east end of the living room. I had laid a fire in the fireplace there but we hadn't had time to light it since moving in.

The fire now blazed away but very soon the room was completely filled with dense smoke. This was how we discovered that the jackdaws, those charming members of the crow family, had developed a fondness for our home in Dooneen. Their nest had quite blocked the chimney. A quiet cup of tea by the fire had to be postponed while we removed the burning embers and cleared the smoke from the house.

I was fortunate in being able to clear the jackdaws' nest from the chimney as easily as I did. Teetering on the roof, with a brisk wind blowing, I fished the nest out with a pair of fire tongs. The nest might have been much farther down, out of reach. Jackdaws drop sticks down a chimney and wherever the sticks lodge they begin to build their nest.

Our household goods had been very well packed in New York. They were contained in six large and strong wooden crates. Inside the crates were many heavy cardboard boxes filled with books, dishes, bedding and the rest.

We cut the cardboard boxes at the corners, flattened them, and used them between the rows in the garden, as a mulch. From the wooden crates we constructed a duck house and a rabbit house.

There are many ways to learn to farm. Mary and I did it largely by reading. We bought some books, borrowed more from the New York Public Library. Mary got all of the relevant bulletins from the United States Department of Agriculture. We also obtained a complete set of bulletins from the Irish Department of Agriculture and Fisheries.

Then we tried it, and learned from experience. Jeremiah

Daly, our neighbor, was invariably kind and helpful in many practical ways, though his method of farming and the advice contained in the books and pamphlets we had read did not always agree.

Mary did more reading than I did and certainly remembered it better. She could quote chapter and verse on most agricultural subjects. Jeremiah often teased her about this. When we would come to him with a problem Jeremiah would get a twinkle in his eye.

"And what does the book say, Mary?" he would ask.

The question wasn't entirely in fun. Jeremiah was willing to learn as well as to teach.

Just as we had concluded from a pretty rational survey of the world's possibilities that Ireland was the place for us, so we had worked out—back in New York and by largely theoretical considerations—what we wanted on our Irish farm. The key idea was balance. If we were to feed ourselves, or come close to it, we must have a balanced diet. On our tiny plot of land, even if somewhat expanded, every operation had to work in balance with every other operation. We had to create a biological network of which we were a living part.

We needed a large and varied garden—larger than anything we could create in the orchard. Besides, the trees there would soon be too big to share the soil with any garden. We also wanted to include fruit of all sorts—tree fruit and bush fruit or "soft fruit" as berry crops are called in the British Isles.

Vegetable protein certainly exists, but we were not vegetarians. We also wanted milk, cheese, eggs—and meat. In one of our talks in our New York penthouse garden, therefore, Mary and I had decided to keep goats, ducks, rabbits and for a bit of honey on the side, bees.

[50]

Once we had a suitable duck house made out of the packing cases our household goods had come in we decided to
begin livestock farming with ducks. From reading a book we
obtained from the New York Public Library we had chosen
Muscovys as the best breed for our purposes. They were said
to be quiet, to graze like geese, to be good layers and excellent
for eating. They had the additional advantage of being willing
to hatch their own eggs and rear their young—as all ducks
were not. Many farmers who raise ducks hatch the eggs under
chickens or use incubators.

Our part of Ireland is geared to cows, pigs and chickens. A
few farmers keep ducks, but not Muscovys. Some had seen
Muscovy ducks and considered them an exotic, useless luxury,
like having peacocks on the lawn.

We put an advertisement for Muscovys in the *Southern Star,*
a weekly newspaper published in Skibbereen. Nothing came
of it. I was about to settle for Indian Runners when Mary got
into a conversation with Sean O'Mahony of Bantry, keen at
shooting snipe and woodcock. Wandering over hills and
moorland, Sean had discovered a lot of things including the
fact that a family named Kingston kept some queer-looking
ducks on their farm the other side of Bantry. These ducks
flew a lot, said Sean, and one of them narrowly missed being
mistaken for suitable game.

We drove to the Kingston farm. Their ducks were indeed
Muscovys. Mary paid for the lot of a dozen or so newly
hatched chicks, to be picked up as soon as they were old
enough to be taken from their mother.

Rats at the Kingston farm ate a few of the ducklings. Some,
of course, turned out to be males, which we ate ourselves as
soon as they were big enough. They were delicious.

The six female Muscovy ducklings were the foundation of our flock. For a duck pond we used a sunken washtub. We still needed an unrelated drake.

We also needed goats, rabbits and bees. And we needed more land.

Communication Means People

⋊ Our greatest need was to close the gap between what we had been and what we were becoming. No doubt this was a task which would take us the rest of our lives and never be completed. Nor was this cause for complaint. The common retirement tragedy of life being finished was not ours to suffer.

Not the least change concerned the important area of human communications. New York City is said to have the best system of communications in the world. We were awakened each morning by a radio news program. Television news and discussion programs were a staple of our intellectual diet. With our breakfast coffee on the terrace we went through the *Wall Street Journal* and the New York *Times*. Later, in our office at the United Nations, we read the Washington *Post* and the St. Louis *Post-Dispatch*.

We had one telephone at home and two at the office. Mary had an automatic recording device at the office to take messages when she was not in. She also had a teletype machine in the pantry, at the apartment. We often used tape recorders for interviews and speeches.

Our work entailed an unceasing discussion of current world affairs. We wanted and perhaps needed to know everything of importance that happened anywhere—and to know it instantly.

When we moved to rural Ireland all of this suddenly had dropped into the North Atlantic. We had no radio in working order, no television—and no telephone. A newspaper subscription was beyond our means.

For a time the St. Louis *Post-Dispatch* was sent to me without charge but that came by surface mail, arriving as much as two months after the day of publication. We did try to look over these old copies. They ended up as mulch in the garden. There they achieved a species of immortality as recycled organic matter.

When we were cut off from communication with the outside world there was a great silence at first. From time to time a feeling close to panic would sweep over me. Anything might be happening in the world and we wouldn't know. Old habits die slowly.

Gradually the silence began to be filled with sounds that reached our ears at first hand, sounds originating in the immediate world around us. The wind blew. The sea lapped the shore. Birds sang. Two miles away the angelus was sounded at the Star of the Sea in Kilcrohane and we could hear the bell toll faintly in Dooneen when the wind was right. A cock crowing, a donkey braying, the hum of bees gathering nectar—these things we heard. We also heard human voices, each identifiable as belonging to a particular person, the meaning often clear even if the words were indistinct—Jeremiah calling to Prince, his dog, as they herded the cattle; Kathleen calling the men to dinner.

Undistracted by flashing lights, swiftly moving automobiles, by the unnamed shadows of a million human figures scurrying by or by the flickering lights and shadows on a television tube we began to see more clearly the things that surrounded us.

We watched tiny shoots bursting through the soil as the seeds we had planted germinated and began to grow. We saw the birds and the flowers in the hedges and began to identify separate species. We noted with special pleasure the dramatic variety of clouds billowing above the mountains and the phases of the moon at night. In the absence of competing light the stars as seen from Dooneen were bright lanterns hung in the sky. In the early morning the sunlight slanted across the buildings in our haggard with a quality of magic in it.

Inevitably Mary and I came to know each other better and each of us discovered inner resources unsuspected in New York.

Our house in Dooneen, as it ceased to become a place for vacations and transformed itself into a permanent home, became an object of wonder and affection. While we were planning the renovation of the house we had had a guest in our New York apartment. She was an attractive young girl but she stayed too long. We decided to remove partitions in our Dooneen house, creating one large living room downstairs, with a fireplace at either end, and a kitchen. The upstairs followed the same plan, with a large bedroom-study and a bathroom. We eliminated a guest room.

Instead, during our final vacation in Dooneen, Anthony McCarthy and his crew had remodeled one of the stone barns for use of our guests. It now contained a bathroom, a closet, and places for five to sleep.

The house itself became intimately ours. It was furnished largely with the things we had brought from our New York apartment. Every corner of the house was familiar, belonging to Mary and me alone.

There was more evidence of prosperity in the whole place than our retirement income would justify. We had prepared it as our permanent home while both of us were working in New York and our joint income was much higher. This anomaly did not go unnoted.

We worked sixteen hours a day as if we were poor—which we were. We worked to eat. But we lived unaccountably well.

Some of our neighbors, I suppose, thought we were rich eccentrics. A few, I think, resented this. One farmer tried to sell us some spoiled hay for use as a garden mulch at approximately five times its real value. He was aggrieved when we refused to pay his price and bought straw from another farmer at a fair rate instead.

On the whole, though, we achieved amazingly good relations inside what was, and is, a tightly knit community. Father Walsh and his excellent young curate, Father Keating, were immensely helpful. We had entertained the local pub keeper, Michael McCarthy, and his wife at our New York apartment.

The real key to our acceptance, though, was the Daly family, our closest neighbors. As we settled down in Dooneen we began to know Jeremiah Daly and his family better.

Physically, Jeremiah and I are opposites. I am tall and lanky, he is shorter, barrel-chested, strong as a bull. We are almost exactly the same age. Despite his West Cork accent and my Yankee accent we communicated well from the outset. One reason may have been that each of us was forced to simplify ideas in order to get them through the accent barrier.

More than most men I have ever known Jeremiah has a firm grasp on his own identity. He knows what he is—an Irish farmer. He knows who he is—Jeremiah of the Daly family, traditional poets in the castles of the O'Mahonys but farmers for many hundreds of years. The colonial experience of Ireland has distorted many Irish personalities, but not Jeremiah's. One reason may have been that this part of Ireland, as remote from Dublin Castle as possible, was never subjugated by the British Raj, except superficially. Jeremiah remains a human being of fierce independence, greeting all men as equals.

He is passionately attached to his own land. His good eighty-eight-acre farm was the gift of an uncle who emigrated to America, worked hard and saved his money so that his nephews could stay home and farm. The uncle never married. I don't know what Jeremiah said to his uncle to thank him, but he has lived his gratitude by being a good farmer. When we first knew the Dalys Jeremiah seldom left the land except to attend Mass at Kilcrohane and to visit the neighborhood pub occasionally. Now the Dalys have a car, driven by his sons, but Jeremiah seldom goes in it farther than Kilcrohane, two miles away.

Indoors and outdoors, winter and summer, Jeremiah mostly wears the same clothes: gum boots, work pants, a shirt and a sweater and a cap on his head and nearly always has a pipe in his mouth. His hands are square and meaty. Before he got the farm Jeremiah trained as a blacksmith but he was never happy away from the land. A life of constant toil has not deadened his appreciation for beauty.

Once Mary and I were walking home from the pub, on a

clear evening, with Jeremiah and Kathleen. As we reached a rise in the road, overlooking the bay, Jeremiah suddenly told us to stop.

"Look!" he said. The full moon was reflected in the bay.

When we were traveling back and forth between Dooneen and New York Jeremiah often would come up to our place when we were away to care for Mary's flowers. He insisted that it was his pleasure to do so. Once he found a wild lily in a field and transplanted it to our haggard. It is still there, now a small bed of lilies.

When we first knew Jeremiah we assumed he was farming on land his father and his father's father had farmed.

"Not at all," he replied, explaining that he was reared on a farm five miles to the west. "I'm a stranger here like yourselves." He had come to Dooneen only thirty-five or forty years before.

Kathleen, Jeremiah's wife, is very sure of herself, as are many rural Irish women. Unlike some she does not dominate her husband. Jeremiah would not be an easy man to dominate in any event. Kathleen was born O'Donovan. Her family lived at the very end of the peninsula, where the gales strike first and hardest.

Kathleen once told me that as a little girl she wanted a doll for Christmas more than anything else in the world. The closest she ever came to getting one was the Christmas her parents gave her an orphaned lamb to care for. The lamb followed Kathleen everywhere. Still she wanted a doll.

One day on her way to the store—a three-mile walk, the lamb following her—she came upon the fragments of a broken religious statue in the ditch. The Virgin had been quite smashed but the Child was still intact. Kathleen picked it up and took it home with her. She hid it, for she feared that to treat the Christ Child as her doll would be a sin, and secretly made baby clothes for it. She did have a doll after all.

With a farm of their own, better than most on the peninsula, though containing patches of rocks, heather and furze, Kathleen and Jeremiah have built a better life than either of their parents knew. Of their five children one daughter had a good education and became a schoolteacher before being married to a boy from the next village, Ahakista, who went into the building business in England and prospered. Another daughter married a neighboring farm boy after a romance while both were working in England. They returned to farm his father's land. One son went to England to work and stayed there. A second son worked at the co-operative creamery in Kilcrohane. A third son, Jerry, worked with Jeremiah on the farm and would inherit it.

The process of choosing the son to inherit the land is a complex one in West Cork. It is, I think, much more rational than merely leaving the farm to the eldest son. Jerry is the third child in point of age and the second son.

In part it is a self-selection process. Jerry liked farming the best.

To be certain that Jerry would be content to stay in Dooneen and farm, his father, Jeremiah, tried an unusual experiment. He arranged with his son-in-law in England to take Jerry on in the building business for a year to see if he did not prefer it. After nine months in England Jerry could stick it no longer and returned home.

I asked him what he had missed most, while in England.

"Tom," he replied with a grin. Tom is the big, friendly white horse who pulls the two-wheeled cart or the plow.

Working together, Tom and Jerry form a close, intimate team. England seemed cold and friendless by comparison.

Jerry is a younger edition of his father, as strong, kind and cheerful. I often hear them talking at their chores when they do not know that I am listening. They work together as equals, respecting each other, friends engaged in a task both enjoy.

One reason for Jeremiah's unusually close relationship with his children may be the fact that for two years, when they were quite young, he was both mother and father to them. Kathleen had fallen and broken a rib, which punctured a lung. Instead of going to a doctor she carried on. Tuberculosis developed and she spent two years in the hospital. Jeremiah washed and ironed the little girls' dresses and baked the brown soda bread every day and also ran the farm, with the help of a hired man.

The process of one generation taking over from another is by no means always accomplished without conflict. There is a tendency for farmers to delay turning over top management to their sons. It is the rural Irish equivalent of middle-class city men resisting retirement. In rural Ireland this can lead to serious mutual resentments.

Nor is rural Ireland, for all its strong sense of community, free from individual, group and family antagonisms. The rural Irish are human like the rest of us.

As Mary and I began to be a part of the complex matrix of rural Irish life, however, we came to understand that even without the myriad of electronic devices that contributed to communications in New York there was a species of communication at work on Muintirvara peninsula that was amazingly efficient. In a sense the mechanistic forms of communica-

tion in New York were only poor substitutes for the human network of communications in rural Ireland.

We accepted Father Walsh's invitation and despite our Protestant backgrounds began attending the Star of the Sea on Sundays and Catholic holidays, along with all of our neighbors. From the pulpit, news of community activities, dances, carnivals, and the availability of seeds and meetings of the growers' co-operative, were given a place alongside Masses, prayers and sermons. Indeed, Father Keating, the curate— himself a farmer's son and a beekeeper of some skill— often included in his sermons sound advice on progressive farm practices.

When the Mass was ended and the packed church was emptied—the people presumably going "to serve and love the Lord"—the men all gathered in groups roughly corresponding to the areas in which they lived. They lit their pipes and discussed all things that came to mind. Since everyone knew where everyone else would be standing—one group in front of the school, another by the pub, a third beside the post office, etc.—it was easy for individuals to cross over and consult men living miles away from their own homesteads. The women, keeping separate from the men outside the church as, for the most part, they did inside, had their own groups for talking.

Weekdays farmers gathered at the co-operative creamery when they brought their milk there in the morning. Every day but Sunday Mick Desmond, the postman, also made his rounds. His transportation was a bicycle and his route covered twenty-two miles west of Kilcrohane.

There were no mailboxes. Mick simply rode his bicycle up to every farmhouse along his route. Barking dogs announced his coming. He entered without knocking, often staying for a cup of tea or other refreshment. As a favor to a few subscribers of the Cork *Examiner,* Mick also delivered the newspaper, reading it along the way himself. He thus kept himself informed on local gossip, by word of mouth, and on national and world events as published in the newspaper, as well.

In addition almost all farmers had radios, on which they got the news morning and night. When we moved to Ireland a few were beginning to get television sets.

The most impressive means of communication remained the constant speech and interaction between human beings. There were no secrets on Muintirvara peninsula, excepting a few kept from the priests and the police, by force of old habit.

A neighbor once advised us to be cautious when talking to these men.

"The police and the priests," he said, "they are not like us."

Mary and I had no secrets to keep and did not mind if all of our guests were noted and identified and if every trip we made away from Dooneen was the subject of general interest. We tried to tell our neighbors about these things as completely as we could; we enjoyed the interest they took and were ourselves interested in what they did.

The advantages of this mutual interest were enormous, as we were to discover. Illness, accident, a need of any sort soon became known. Mutual help followed mutual interest.

Land Hunger

Rocks and cutout peat bogs are at no premium on Muintirvara peninsula but good farmland is a rare and precious thing. A well-drained field with a good depth of rich topsoil and a southern exposure is given loving care. It is called a kind field. If in grass, such a field is green the year around.

You could read in the *Irish Farmers' Journal* that good farmland in Ireland was worth three hundred pounds an acre, or about $720. What Mary and I needed, and needed desperately, was not a statistical average Irish farm acre but a good garden plot, preferably adjoining our place, and some suitable land where goats could browse.

As usual with all our problems we took this one first to Jeremiah. He understood our needs. Unfortunately he had no good farmland to spare. With greatest difficulty Mary had induced him to add two very small pieces of good land to our original purchase, straightening our north border. Adjoining those plots Jeremiah had a fine field which we knew he could not sell. A part of it was planted in a permanent cash crop of daffodils.

To the south of our place was Jeremiah's own haggard. To the west was a tiny plot, stony and flooded by a spring. It belonged to an Englishwoman who had bought the house which we had looked at before we bought our house from Jeremiah.

We wanted the tiny plot to the west mostly because it was an enclave in our own place. The Englishwoman agreed to sell it. Jerry Daly joined in making an oral bargain—from which she later withdrew. Whether we might have been able to make a garden there was very doubtful in any case.

This left the fine pasture to the east, which we had admired from the outset. It belonged to Michael McCarthy, the pub keeper, who also farmed. Even before we moved to Dooneen we had begun a long series of conversations with him on the subject of that field. These conversations usually took place in Michael's pub. This gave him both a tactical and a financial advantage, for it meant buying refreshments for ourselves and for whatever farmers happened to drop in to watch the bargaining.

There was much good-natured banter. The subject of money was avoided with care. In the end Michael would repeat that we were talking about his best field and it was not for sale.

Observing our frustration Jeremiah at one point rather diffidently mentioned that he had one field down toward the sea which he had been unable to use for anything. About nine acres in extent, it was called a mountain pasture, not for any elevation above sea level but because it was wild and uncultivated, full of heather, furze, bracken and in the low places rushes and coarse grass unsuitable for cows. No one had been able to figure out how to drain the field and in winter it was very wet.

So desperate was our land hunger that Mary and I asked an Irish Department of Agriculture adviser to look over Jeremiah's mountain land to see if any part of it could be made into a garden. He brought with him a borer for making soil tests. He was unable to use it, striking bedrock within an inch or two. The man from the Department of Agriculture advised us to forget Jeremiah's rocky field.

Finally we steeled ourselves and made an offer for the three-acre field that Michael owned, to the east of our place. We said we would give him a thousand pounds for the land, a hundred pounds above the top market price.

Michael countered by saying that the field was not really farmland but a potential building site. There might even be oil beneath the land, he added, as prospecting for oil was going on off the coast of Ireland. We listened patiently. Perhaps he might sell us some portion of the field? Michael would think about that.

After we had moved to Dooneen permanently we renewed the talk about land with Michael. He was ready for us. He offered to sell a quarter of an acre of his field for 500 pounds, about $1,200. This was well over three times the market value for the best Irish farmland.

We staked out a quarter of an acre immediately adjoining our orchard and discussed it with Liam Collins, the solicitor. He frowned and made clicking noises but we all had to admit that we badly needed the land. We paid the price and got it.

The garden plot overlooked the little fort which had given Dooneen its name. Surveying our new purchase we felt certain the farmer who had lived in the fort some three thousand years ago also had tilled our garden. Indeed, when we cut through the hedge separating our orchard from the new field we found there a stone containing fragments of an inscription in ogham, ancient Irish writing resembling cuneiform—chiseled slashes of unequal length.

Meanwhile we got on with the business of living in Dooneen. In the orchard our little vegetable garden was flourishing. The ducks seemed happy in their packing-box duck house—and even happier while wandering through the orchard garden. There they picked up slugs—but also nibbled the lettuce somewhat too much. I built a chickenwire fence around the orchard and the ducks wandered elsewhere.

We had read enough about goats to know that a decent milk yield could be expected only with pedigreed stock from a good milk line. We had written the Irish Department of Agriculture in Dublin but had received no reply. We called them on the telephone. Someone in the department thought there was a herd of milk goats in the vicinity of Dublin. We decided to drive up and see for ourselves.

By this time we had long relinquished our motorbikes in favor of a van—a panel truck on a passenger-car body. It was in this that we drove to Dublin. We had a double purpose in going there.

Trying to find good milch goats in Ireland was one thing. Even more, Mary and I were anxious about our friend Gordon Clark and wanted to see him. The last time he had visited us in Dooneen he had planted several trees and had complained of a pain in one leg while doing so. Such a complaint was quite unlike him. Obviously it hurt a lot. Now Gordon was in a Dublin hospital.

We had come to think of Gordon as our best friend in Ireland. It was a friendship that took several years to develop. In New York, where we had known him first, Gordon was just another of the visiting Irish. We were surprised, and a little embarrassed, when he sent us as wedding gifts a set of Waterford glassware and, for Mary, an authentic old Kinsale cloak.

On our trips to Ireland we saw more of him and got to know him better in his own setting. He was an enthusiastic gardener at his home in Greystones, in County Wicklow, a suburb of Dublin. He took considerable vicarious pleasure in our own efforts in a much more remote section of Ireland, and a section that was held in great affection by Gordon.

He knew rural Ireland better than any Dubliner I have met. At one stage in his career he had helped organize young farmers all over the country. He had done many other things, never quite making a serious career out of anything. He was a fine writer, though too diffident to allow himself to become well known outside a limited circle. He also was a publisher. He took a deep interest in Irish Georgian architecture and indeed was himself something of an eighteenth-century man.

He was a fine conversationalist. In Dooneen we had spent many happy evenings with him before the fire. Gordon was a deeply religious Catholic. This fact infused his talk but did not limit it. Whatever the subject, he would take his pipe out of his mouth, smile and make some pithy contribution that was both informative and amusing.

We had seen Gordon on our previous trips to Dublin and had watched him struggle against an illness that obviously was serious, though we did not, then, know its full gravity. It was difficult to think that our old companion would never again visit us in Dooneen.

On the way to Dublin we stopped for lunch with Father

Walsh. To our sorrow he had been transferred from Muintirvara Parish to Blackrock, a Cork City suburb. We saw him there and enjoyed the visit—too much, for we delayed our departure.

It was getting late, so we stopped at a Tourist Board office between Cork and Dublin and made a hotel reservation. We chose a place called Hotel Montrosa because it was in North Dublin, fairly convenient to the hospital where Gordon was and also to the farm outside Dublin where we hoped to find milch goats.

Approaching Dublin in the van, at about Naas, fog and darkness closed in together. The rest of the journey was at a snail's pace and dangerous and nerve-racking enough at that. Our host at the Montrosa, a retired football star named John Egan, was surprised that we got there at all.

The next morning when we saw Gordon we were shocked by his appearance. Only the wasted shell of our dear friend was left. There was no talk of plans after his release from the hospital—plans which earlier had included the purchase of a vacation home in West Cork, perhaps not far from Dooneen. We had brought him six pears from our own trees. Later we learned that he had not had the appetite to eat them.

Mary and I left Gordon with a feeling of sadness. We talked about it as we drove through Phoenix Park, to find the goat farm. The fog persisted. The great trees in the park were like giant ghosts looming out of the gloom.

We inquired of a man working on telephone lines where the goat farm might be. The Department of Agriculture had given us a name but only a very vague idea of the location. The telephone man suggested we try a nearby estate.

There was a long driveway, through a break in a high wall.

Every few yards along the drive was a sign urging all and sundry to keep out. Beware the guard dogs, one sign said. Another offered the intelligence that the estate was electrically protected, leaving much to the imagination.

We saw or heard no dogs. When we reached the farmyard it was completely deserted. I knocked on the door and no one responded.

As I was entering the van to leave I heard footsteps behind me and out of the fog came a man with a sack of something across his back. He answered my questions about goats with few words, and these spoken with a thick German accent. He himself had no goats.

"There once was a man near here," he added, "who did keep goats. He had a woman at his place who took baths in the milk."

There had been some scandal in the newspapers, he said. Now he believed the people had moved away.

We tried other houses in the neighborhood. People remembered that the goats had nibbled the hedges. There was much speculation about the woman who bathed in goats' milk, a story all had heard. We found no goats.

Information concerning rabbits turned out to be a little better in the Department of Agriculture. Following their advice we found a rabbit breeder. Although he had no rabbits for sale at the moment he promised to send along five breeding does and an unrelated buck as soon as they were old enough. The delay in getting rabbits was fortunate because I had not yet built cages for them.

We drove home empty-handed, but were glad enough to get there. Dooneen at the end of August is full of magic, with low clouds floating over the mountains and fog banks rolling

down into the valleys. There are spider webs in the hedges that glisten in the morning dew. Red fuchsia blossoms hang in the still air.

Making the rabbit cages was a tedious business with much twisting and bending of welded wire mesh. We had no real model to work from, only various photographs in books and pamphlets on keeping rabbits. Housing for the rabbit cages—like the duck house—had been constructed of used packing cases.

The rabbits arrived by train in Cork City. I picked them up at the station there and drove them to Dooneen. They seemed to like their new cages. This was to be our chief source of meat—though I had yet to nerve myself to kill rabbits and was not looking forward to that with any pleasure. The five does had first to be bred by the buck, the young rabbits reared to maturity. Calculations on the amount of rabbit meat one could produce were fabulous—on paper.

Mary and I fenced the new garden plot ourselves, buying oak fence posts at the co-operative creamery in Kilcrohane. We used sheep wire, with one strand of barbed wire and some chickenwire at the bottom to discourage rabbits and badgers. I am still surprised that it has kept Michael's cows out of the garden. It has not kept out wild rabbits and badgers entirely but has reduced such raids to acceptable proportions.

Father Keating, while curate in Kilcrohane, had kept bees. Like Father Walsh he had been transferred to another parish —to Ballydehob, some thirty miles distant. We telephoned him for advice on obtaining bees.

"Don't do anything," he replied. "I will bring the bees." Weeks went by and we heard no more.

We had been living in Dooneen for a month and felt that we had made some progress. We had worked very hard. In a sense, though, we still lacked the fundamental ingredient of our little agricultural enterprise—a couple of good milch goats to help feed us and to furnish fertilizer for the garden.

Gales, Lambs and a Kitten

❧ The first gale struck early that year, before the middle of September. Two years before, but much later in the year, we had experienced a gale while making our first winter visit to Dooneen. Mary's mother was with us and the gale had struck while we were driving from Shannon Airport.

I realized that it was indeed a full gale only when I noticed furze bushes blowing horizontally across the road as we topped the pass over MacGillycuddy's Reeks. Before we reached Glengarriff, on Bantry Bay, a tree blew down in front of us, blocking the road. We managed to find a back road through the forest there but it was well after dark before we drove out Muintirvara peninsula.

In the wild excitement of the gale a cow slid over a hedge in front of us and our head lamp collided with the cow's horn. The cow was unhurt but not the head lamp.

As usual, the gale blew for two more days before it subsided. Mary and I floundered around in the wind, retrieving black plastic sheeting that was stripped off the orchard, securing what we could secure. There was a feeling of adventure in it for us, then, though I found myself awake at night, wondering if the roof would hold.

It was this vague sense of dread that stayed with me as we experienced our first gale while living in Dooneen. By then we had ducks and rabbits in makeshift houses. Whether they would stand a high wind was a question.

No one, living on the wild seacoast of southwestern Ireland, takes a gale lightly. When we first bought our place and were using it for vacations we talked of living here the year around; Jeremiah said he wondered if we would like the winter gales. A few of our neighbors have left Ireland altogether, for America, England or Australia, because they had wearied of listening to the wind blowing day after day and night after night at gale force. This does not happen too often, perhaps six to a dozen times a year.

We remain dependent on Jeremiah to tell us when a gale will blow. His judgment is more reliable than weather reports from Dublin or London. On a quiet day he will look at a gray sky, with a vague mist on the horizon, and say: "We'll have a gale, I'd be thinking." I have never known him to be wrong.

The wind, that first September, began blowing before the rains came. "It's a dry wind that does the harm," said Jeremiah. We listened to it roar. All of our fruit trees had been staked and tied as we planted them. Now Mary and I retied the trees, twice the normal effort because we were fighting the wind while we worked.

We put up the heavy board shutters over the front of the rabbit house. The ducks were still out and we left them for the moment, passively facing the wind, depending on their own streamlining to preserve them from its fury. Later we would feed them and put them inside the duck house but they would go only reluctantly, perhaps bewildered by the wind.

Technically, of course, a gale is a wind of a certain velocity, but in the language of our neighbors it is any strong wind, mighty in gusts, blowing usually for three days and nights. The sky is dark. There is a cruelty in it. In the unrelenting assault of the wind anxiety mounts toward panic. Roof slates seem awfully vulnerable. Trees and shrubs whip and bend. There is a terrible noise as the wind roars between houses and outbuildings, over hedges and through trees. The sea itself gives out an angry howl.

After the dry wind had blown for several hours that mid-September the rains began. The lashing of the rain against windows and doors, against the earth itself was a new sound. Nothing can hold out entirely against this driving rain. It seeps through windows, under doors, into walls. One understands why seacoast farmers prize a sheltered position for a house or field, why stone hedges were erected and planted to break the wind.

Mary and I, like all farmers, found ourselves out in this rain and wind from time to time, tending ducks and rabbits, checking trees and buildings. No matter how one dresses in rain gear for such tasks the beating rain finds an opening. One returns to the fire, indoors, cold and wet. Still it is better to go out, to face the gale. To stay huddled indoors, waiting in vain for the wind to subside, is to court madness.

Incidents of a gale are a part of the common pub talk and haggard conversation. There are stories of boats that went down, of roofs that were blown away. One who is a little queer in the head is said to have a slate missing.

A gale blew in the stone wall of the Dalys' turf shed, next

door. It was a stout building that had stood for several hundred years and once was used as a cabin where an Irish family lived. Wind and rain finally washed away the clay that held the stones in place and the wall fell. Jerry Daly quickly rebuilt it, saving the building, working while the wind blew.

There was a crisis of sorts during that first mid-September gale that caused much amusement though it was a near enough thing to tragedy. Anthony McCarthy owned a fishing boat, a large, open vessel. He kept it at Dooneen pier, just below our place, the bow tied to the pier itself, the stern tied to a bollard on a rock offshore. When Anthony's sister, a nun, came home on leave from the convent it was her pleasure to have Anthony take her fishing in the boat.

A farmer's wife, using a pair of binoculars, was scanning the bay and the fields nearby during that September gale, when she noticed Anthony's boat dancing about. The rope which had fastened it to the pier had parted.

Word reached Anthony soon enough, communications on the peninsula being what they are. A crowd, including Anthony, gathered on the pier. He tried to grasp the boat with a grappling hook, thrown out from the pier, but the distance was too great and the target moving too rapidly.

Anthony does not swim. Few do on the peninsula, even those who make a part of their living by fishing. The idea of diving into the bay in such a wind would not occur to them in any event.

Precisely this idea did occur to an Englishman who happened to be there. Before anyone knew what he was about he had stripped off his clothes; at the last minute Anthony succeeded in tying a rope about his waist. Then the Englishman dived in.

He was a man past middle age. In former years and under other circumstances he might have been able to swim through the angry waters and rescue the boat. As it was, they had to haul him in with the rope and he crawled back on the pier, blue with cold and nearly exhausted.

Later the boat was saved by using a rubber dinghy, also tethered by a rope, and manned by an experienced boatman.

When the gale had spent its force nature smiled again. Our duck and rabbit houses had withstood the wind. There was, after all, much of summer weather left. Warned of the winter to come, though, we went to work putting more and more food in the very large deep freeze we had brought with us from America. In August we had picked quantities of blackberries from the hedges, packaged these, and put them in the freezer. To these we had added some herring, purchased from local fishermen, and a few chickens bought from neighbors.

We had seen sheep grazing in common pasturage on the mountain behind our house. We learned that Jim Tobin, who lived at the end of the peninsula, was rounding up his mountain lambs. After several conferences after Mass in Kilcrohane we arranged to obtain two of these lambs, now fairly big, as an added meat supply.

For some reason that escapes me Jim Tobin wanted us to pick up the lambs in our van at night, and a very foggy night at that. Noel Daly went with me, for I was picking up a lamb for the Daly family as well. Noel's eyes and mine barely were able to pick out the edge of the road, in the fog, and we managed to avoid the steep drop to the ocean. It was a nervous journey for the lambs and for ourselves as well.

Mary and I shut our two lambs in the goat-less goat house

for the night. The next morning we tethered them at the end of the orchard, where a bit of grass was growing. Mary and I will try many things but at that point killing and dressing out two large lambs seemed beyond our capacities. We decided to take the problem to the pub.

Pub discussions may not sound very useful at the time. Too many people talk at once. There are interludes of song about Ireland's heroic past. Surprisingly, more often than not something does come of all this.

In this case it was Tim O'Sullivan, a farmer neighbor, who came out to see us the next day, singing as he came. He had, he said, been to the Bantry cattle fair and there had met an old friend named Thomas Ward, a farmer living near Durrus who also operated a slaughterhouse. Tim had discussed our problem with Ward—called Thos., pronounced "Toss"—and he had agreed to kill, skin and dress the lambs.

"So come along, Donal," said Tim, dropping the final *d* of my first name as the Irish do, and still quite happy from the time he had at the Bantry cattle fair. "You and I will take the lambs to Thos. Ward."

So Tim and I loaded the lambs in the van and were off, stopping at a pub or two on the way. The following day I returned to Thos. Ward's place and picked up the carcasses and the skins.

Mary and I cut the carcasses into suitable pieces, using a bulletin published by the United States Department of Agriculture as a guide. I held the book and read aloud from it while Mary used the knife, cleaver and hacksaw. Then we packaged the result and it, too, went into the freezer.

Of an evening, often late, when such a job was done, Mary

and I would sit around the fire and plan the next day's work. Two companions in such moments were Prince and Padraic. Prince was the Dalys' cow dog. Padraic was our own cat.

We had developed a warm friendship with Prince while still using Dooneen only for vacations. He never forgot us between trips. When we came to Dooneen to live Prince made it a habit to come in and sit with us by the fire of evenings, when his work with the cows was done. The relationship between Prince and Padraic, the cat, was not the usual cat-and-dog affair.

Padraic had been born at the farm of Mick Desmond, the postman. Mick gave him to Michael McCarthy, the pub keeper who took him to his barn to learn from the older cats how to catch mice and rats. Instead, Padraic caught the hoof of a cow squarely in the middle of his very small tummy.

We had the kitchen door open one day and Padraic stumbled in. He was more than half dead, having dragged himself from Michael's barn, a half a mile away.

Mary examined him. Padraic lay down, moaning. Fortunately, at that moment Mary looked out the window and saw that the veterinary surgeon was visiting the Dalys to look after a cow. She took Padraic down there immediately. A shot of penicillin saved his life. The vet said Padraic had a full-blown case of peritonitis from the kick of the cow.

From that moment Padraic was our cat. He was a very small creature, all black and white, but he knew what he wanted—which was to stay alive and to remain as close to Mary and me as he could.

Padraic had just recovered from the peritonitis when one of the Dalys' cats, a tom named Timmy, seeing a rival male growing up in the neighborhood, attacked him viciously. Padraic's belly was ripped wide open. This time we used oral penicillin but the problem of the open wound remained.

Prince came into the house and took a look at Padraic. It was by no means the first cat Prince had seen. In the Dalys' barn Prince had had a very good cat friend; the two often curled up to sleep together on a chilly night. Prince's cat friend, though, had been killed by the same Timmy who had attacked Padraic. Prince never forgave Timmy for that.

His sympathy for Padraic was immediate. Evening after evening he and Padraic would lie together by the fire. Sometimes they slept. Sometimes Prince gently would lick Padraic's wounded belly.

When Prince would go home to his barn Padraic would come up to the bedroom with Mary and me. There, while still very ill, he would sleep on my pillow, beside my head. In the middle of the night I would feel out for him, not sure whether he was still alive. Padraic would purr to reassure me.

After Padraic recovered I caught a severe case of the flu and had to go to bed. Padraic returned to my pillow to purr for my encouragement.

When we both were well Padraic would lie beside me when I was writing. More than once I thought of the ancient Irish poem by a writer-monk about his cat, beginning: "I and Pangur Ban my cat,/ 'Tis a like task we are at:/ Hunting mice is his delight,/ Hunting words I sit all night."

The friendship between Padraic and Prince never faltered.

Whenever Prince thought Padraic was in danger, whether from Timmy or any other source, Prince would come to his rescue. As Padraic grew up he and Prince finally chased Timmy away altogether and he took up residence in the barn

of a neighbor about a mile away. The farmer was fortunate. Despite his vicious nature, or perhaps because of it, Timmy was a fine ratter.

Prince, a typical collielike Irish cattle dog, is handsome, intelligent and gentle. Not only does he stop fights between cats, or between cats and dogs, but if two bull calves square off to fight in a field Prince will run out to separate them.

Once when Michael's cows strayed into our haggard Prince answered Mary's call. Though Mary had never directed Prince to handle cattle before and a strange herd was involved, Prince skillfully got Michael's cows back out into the road and on down to Michael's field. Prince's Irish ear apparently was not confused by Mary's strange, Yankee accent.

Two Goats in Kid

October was as glorious a month as the English poets, writing in another part of the British Isles to be sure, had said it was. Mary and I drove in our van the length of Ireland to pick up two milch goats, Fleur and Katrina, at Finlarig Farm, near Ballynahinch, in County Down. Blackbirds wheeled against a sky of blue with white clouds billowing. Ruined castles stood sentinel on either side. Trees wore their autumn colors. Streams tumbled down rocks, sparkling. It was a trip to delight any scenery-seeking tourist.

The Irish Department of Agriculture in Dublin helped us find the goats after all, telephoning their counterparts in Belfast as if the border were not there. The Northern Ireland Department of Agriculture directed us to Finlarig. The goats were Saanens, a Swiss breed adopted by the English. The goat farm was operated by two unmarried women, one English, one Irish. They also had English cocker spaniel dogs. Mary sat before the fire, there, with one of the cocker puppies on her lap and fell in love. I said, no, we had problems enough.

[85]

"When I was a child I had a cocker puppy," said Mary, "and he was run over by an automobile . . ." I maintained a churlish silence.

Both of the goats were in kid. Fleur was larger than Katrina. It was a slow journey home. The two goats insisted on standing in the van, behind us. Katrina nibbled my left ear. I drove slowly so they would not be upset and we stopped in the Irish Midlands to pick up a Muscovy drake, by previous arrangement. We arrived late in Dooneen.

At last we had goats in the goat house. We tried putting them in the fine bit of pasture we had purchased from Michael McCarthy. The goats nibbled the hedges but were little interested in the grass. We fed them hay and concentrates—oats, bran, flaked maize, soya bean meal. They needed pasturage.

Evenings we read up on goats, having obtained two new books on the subject on our trip north. The more we read the more we thought of the rough mountain land that Jeremiah had offered to sell us. The things that grew there were not much use for cattle but seemed just right for goats.

Jeremiah sold us seven acres for seven hundred pounds, a fair price for the sort of land it was. Foreigners without an Irish connection were limited to five acres of arable land. The authorities had to be satisfied that this was not. This caused one long delay. We also had to wait for several months before we could get fencing material and a crew to put it up. Our own experience with fencing the garden plot purchased from Michael convinced us that fencing the mountain, with little but rocks to support the posts, was beyond us.

With Jeremiah's generous permission we did not wait for legal ownership or for the fence. We began taking the goats to the mountain pasture and sitting with them while they grazed.

Strangers to goats, Mary and I went together at first to sit with them. It would, we thought, take both of us to keep them from straying.

What we had overlooked is that goats are animals with a strong herd instinct. The way to handle goats is to become honorary members of the herd. It is an inside job.

Once your herd membership is established, all that is required is to be there in the pasture with them. They stay nearby because goats like to keep together. If they should wander off, forgetfully following the growth of heather, all that is necessary is to call out and they will return. Any sound will do. Sometimes I brought my alto recorder to the pasture and practiced while the goats grazed.

Once we discovered how easy it was, Mary and I took turns goat-sitting. One of us could then work in the garden.

I found it a fine, lonely job out there on the mountain. I read. Even in winter I burrowed into the furze bushes and slept.

Mostly I found it a time to smoke my pipe, look about me and enjoy my own thoughts and fantasies.

I learned a bit about goats by watching them. Fleur was a bully without conscience. Whenever Katrina would find an especially lush lot of heather Fleur would go after it, knocking Katrina out of the way with an imperious toss of the head.

Goats do not just graze along, like cows in a good pasture. They pick and choose—a leaf here, a bit of grass there, a furze blossom, a heather plant. Mary and I both found ourselves looking at growing things everywhere with goats' eyes.

"Oh," Mary would say as we drove along in the van on a trip to Bantry, "that would make a delicious bit for Fleur and Katrina." If we had picked up someone along the road to ride

with us in the back of the van, as we often did, explanations were called for. The rural Irish are tolerant of eccentricity.

Alone with the goats in their pasture I would pick out a sunny rock to sit on. After watching the goats for a time my attention would turn to the pasture itself. You could see where the last bit of turf had been stripped for burning. Two great ridges of rock, formed by the folding of the earth's crust in some past geological period, transversed the pasture from east to west. Along the sides of these rock ridges heather grew and in the valleys, furze, bracken and brambles.

I could identify at least three different kinds of heather. They bloomed at different seasons, which was fortunate, because the goats especially liked the blossoms. Furze, also called gorse, is a prickly green bush. It bears yellow-gold flowers resembling sweet peas and blooms the year around. "When the furze stops blooming, kissing is out of season," is a local aphorism. Bracken is a fern, growing waist-high in the shelter of the rock outcrops. Brambles, blackberry canes gone wild, were scattered among the bracken. Aside from all these were many small plants, tiny flowers like jewels and at least a dozen varieties of grass.

Birds flew above the pasture—tiny stonechats, which made a noise like two pebbles struck together, and kestrels, falcons which flew against the wind but with exactly the same speed as the wind blew so that they remained stationary in reference to the ground as they looked for insects and mice. Robins and thrushes sat atop the furze bushes and sang.

When I looked out over the open Atlantic, to the west, occasionally I would see a large ship passing the mouth of the bay, a reminder that out there somewhere the world of industry, commerce, finance and politics still bustled along. I remembered what life had been like when I was younger, the bright lights of New York, London, Paris, Rio de Janeiro, Buenos Aires, Moscow, Cairo. City lights.

I was here, now, sitting on a rock on the lower slopes of an Irish mountain by the sea. Whatever passing moments of regret I might feel could not last long with the wind blowing fresh and the birds singing. From plants and other animals my thoughts turned to mankind as a species.

Somehow in New York, even in our penthouse garden, we seldom thought of ourselves as one among many kinds of animals subsisting on earth. Here in Dooneen mankind was in the minority. Insects were most numerous here, as everywhere in the world. (The weight of the world's insects, I am told, is greater than that of all the other animals together, elephants included.) I wouldn't be surprised if there are as many foxes on Muintirvara peninsula as there are people. Certainly there are many more cows and pigs.

Mostly, though, there are open spaces and clean air, sunshine and rain, green pastures, mountains and sea. There is plenty of elbowroom for every sort of animal life, human life included. No one is crowded. This may be the most important difference of all between life in Dooneen and in the teeming cities of the world. Still, we are all—badgers, hares and human beings—conscious of our neighbors here. They are important to us.

The people on Muintirvara peninsula have a special sense of solidarity as members of the same species huddled together in a wild place where strong winds blow in from the sea. Families anyway have lived as neighbors for a long time. It is different when the family across the way has just moved in from Pittsburgh and when they have lived there for seven hundred years. Many interests are shared: love, hate, friendship and gossip; farming and religion; hopes, fears and history; delight in a field of flowers, a warm fire, a good meal or a day's work well done.

Even if men and women are not always happy with each other here they do not ignore each other. A few may try, but they really do not succeed. The sort of impersonal isolation, of alienation that exists in cities is rare or unknown.

Nor are people isolated from the natural setting. Grass grows, cows eat the grass, farmers milk the cows. It is all a

visible process. Potatoes and cabbages grow in the garden and
are seen to grow. They are harvested, cooked and eaten. The
fire that cooks the food and warms the house is a fire to be
seen, burning turf.

Life is whole. Maybe it begins somewhere up there in the
sky, where clouds billow by day and stars shine by night. Life
includes the worms in the earth and the seals that swim in
Dunmanus Bay, so human-seeming that a thousand mermaid
stories have been told of them. Or is it that life has no beginning and no end, but is a process, a struggle, a becoming? But
when a man and a woman find their way to bed when the
night falls early in winter it is a good life. It is good when a
baby lies in its cradle and looks at the world with wondering
eyes.

Somehow, on Muintirvara peninsula, it all fits together.
Animal droppings fertilize the land, plants grow, animals eat
the plants. The cycle renews itself, the earth turns, the stars
change their patterns as the seasons change.

Death, too, is a part of the cycle of life. Sitting on my rock,
smoking my pipe, I recall the first Irish wake Mary and I had
attended while still only vacationists in Dooneen. It was an
old woman who had died and we joined in the prayers as she
lay there, with candles. Friends and relations of the old woman
ate and drank and talked. Voices were natural, unhushed.
The talk ranged over the life of the woman who had died and
of the community as a whole, yesterday and today. The gap
left by death had begun to close before the wake was over.

The next day there was the funeral Mass and they buried
her in the cemetery at Kilcrohane where the ruins of a
fourteenth-century church are. It is a lovely spot, between the
mountains and the sea.

St. Cruachan built a cell there, they say, and meditated. In the sixth or seventh century that was. When the village was founded it took the name of St. Cruachan and telescoped history, assuming that the church was his, though it was built seven hundred years after the saint had abandoned his cell. Kilcrohane means the church of St. Cruachan.

Fiddling with history does not change the facts of aging and death. We, too, will die. I remember Father Walsh telling me—one day when he came along for a cup of coffee and a chat while Mary and I were working in the haggard—that rural Ireland is a good place in which to grow old. Maybe he meant that growing old can be something not altogether to be regretted, himself growing old as he spoke. Age has its compensations and enjoyments.

So I got up from my rock and brought the goats back to their house, close by our house, overlooking the sea. As I walked the goats browsed the hedges, snipping at the bramble leaves. When we rounded the last turn we could see the two farmhouses, Jeremiah's and ours, and the green fields around them.

This was Ireland. So much has been written about Ireland, so little of it relevant to our own experience. They say it is a place where men like to fight, but we have known chiefly kindness. They say it is a place of fantasy, sentimentality, where people believe in fairies and ghosts. The country Irish we knew were, for the most part, hardheaded realists.

What throws strangers off, I think, is that Ireland is almost what you think it is, but not quite. It is a part of Europe, but on the outer edge, like Russia, a separate thing, a thing in itself.

St. Patrick, so it is said, thought of himself as a Roman. He brought Latin to Ireland as well as Christianity. Most of the Irish, however, continued to speak their old, pagan language. They speak more English now, but an English that often is a translation of the old Irish, with colorful phrases peculiar to itself. Maybe if you can scratch a Russian and find a Tartar you also may scratch an Irishman in this most Christian country and find a Druid.

Dublin is not Ireland. It was Danish, early on, and later very English. Ireland is in the hills and along the seashores, in the green valleys and the dark glens. It is sitting by a turf fire on a misty day, talking and listening.

This was Gordon Clark's Ireland, too. Now we received a cryptic telegram that Gordon had died of cancer of the spine. We had been expecting the sad news. We felt lonely at his death.

It was November when I drove the little van to Dublin to attend Gordon's funeral. It was a solemn and impressive service, the funeral Mass. There was a large crowd.

At Glasnevin Cemetery the rain drizzled out of a dull sky. After Gordon was buried I walked over to the grave of Michael Collins. Then a few of Gordon's friends had come together but there was no proper wake. The sense of loneliness persisted.

I drove back to Dooneen alone. Mary had stayed behind to care for the animals. Only when I passed Durrus and saw again the sunlight sparkling on Dunmanus Bay did my depression lift. Though it was now November the birds in Dooneen were singing as if it were spring.

Settling Down

↘ Man, the hunter, has one set of relationships with nature; man, the tiller of the soil, another. Pre-agricultural man probably has a more intimate feeling for fauna and for the natural flora covering of the earth. Agricultural man certainly has a closer relationship with the earth itself, the soil he tills. There is, I suppose, no other way of developing this relationship with the earth except by grubbing in it, with a persistency born of necessity.

Shortly after I returned from Dublin, and the funeral for Gordon Clark, Mary and I walked out after breakfast one day and looked over the expensive quarter of an Irish acre that we had purchased from Michael McCarthy. We admired the fence we had erected. The grass had grown taller in the fenced-in portion of the larger pasture; Michael's cows looked over the fence with greedy brown eyes.

We had sprinkled basic slag on our new garden site as a gesture toward the future, like baptizing a baby. The serious work on the land had yet to be done.

We had purchased a garden power tool called a Merry Tiller, a machine one walked behind but which itself was powered by a little gasoline engine. For digging up the soil it proved to be extremely useful, covering more ground quicker and better and with less effort than a hand spade.

First, though, our newly fenced-in garden plot must be plowed. Sod on the old pasture was thick and toughly matted with grass roots.

In addition to the rotovator attachment for the Merry Tiller we had purchased with it a set of rubber-tired wheels and a plow. This equipment, theoretically, could be used to convert the machine into one capable of turning the sod. There was something of a gap between theory and practice.

In order to apply sufficient power to the plow to turn the sod it proved necessary for me to assist the little machine with my shoulder. As I finished each row, sweating and panting, it occurred to me that I had retired in good time; a few years more and such an effort would be too much.

Mary suggested with some sense that we might better hire the field plowed by a man with a horse or a proper tractor. That I did not accept this suggestion was due, I like to think, to more than mere stubbornness. It was our land and I wanted to work it myself.

As the plow failed to turn over the sod completely we followed the machine work with a good deal of handwork, turning the sods. When the field was fairly well plowed we had three trailer-loads of cow dung hauled in and we spread it out on the new garden plot. Giving it some time to wash in, we then rotovated the garden. The sods had begun to rot; the rotovator chopped up the sods, carrying on where the plow had left off. Before the field was ready to plant we worked it over with spade, hoe and garden rake and with our bare hands.

In the process we learned something of the land. The soil was excellent to a depth of two or three feet. It contained a good many rocks and small stones and many pottery fragments.

While working the land I read a book on the geology of Ireland, talked to our neighbors and to local historians. We also entertained a group of graduate students of geology who were studying the rocks of our area. I was able to reduce the story of what had happened to create the soil we were tilling to a simplified chronological sequence.

After the earth's crust had cooled it was covered by water, which deposited an overlay of what became sandstone and shale. Movements of the earth's crust distorted the surface, creating great folds, including the mountain ridge now forming the spine of Muintirvara peninsula. The various strata of rocks were exposed in the process.

Erosion further changed the landscape, softening the hills. Then came the glaciers, both cutting the surface and making their own deposits as they melted. Many of the rocks and stones in our garden, apparently, were left there by melting glaciers. The stones remained because they were not much broken up by frosts in our warm corner of Europe.

In addition to the stones the glaciers dumped some good soil, unevenly distributed; our garden was favored. Streams eroding the mountain spine deposited more soil.

In the soil, a succession of plants grew. In time there was a forest covering, including both oak and pine trees. We still find stumps of these trees deep in the peat bogs. The forest floor accumulated a deep bed of rotted leaves—humus, which continues to nourish our garden.

The next stage was the removal of the forest covering. No doubt prehistoric peoples—perhaps including those who had lived in the little fort of Dooneen, less than a hundred yards from our garden—had begun the process as they turned from hunting and fishing to farming. The English completed the deforestation.

As the land was cleared it was tilled by Irish farmers. Some fields around us have been tilled for a thousand years. I am inclined to think our garden has been worked for that long, judging from the age of some of the shards in it. As the land was tilled the humus content was augmented by seaweed hauled up from the shore, by animal dung and—as suggested by the shards—by household wastes. The end result was very good soil indeed, both in our new garden and in the little field we had planted as an orchard.

On our arrival in August, we had planted a temporary vegetable garden in the orchard. We were harvesting cabbage, kale and carrots from it well into the new year. We put quantities of mustard greens into the freezer. Lettuce and radishes were welcome additions to our table.

During one of our winter vacations, before we moved to Dooneen, we had planted a herb garden in the haggard. It flourished. Rosemary, thyme, sage, lavender, chives, parsley, mint, balm and garlic grew into a small forest before our door, filling the air with good odors.

We ate well. No grocery store in any city could have provided the food we grew or gathered in the hedges and fields.

Always a good cook, Mary excelled herself in Dooneen. Hot biscuits, seasoned with rosemary from the haggard, were delicious with tea. Bramble pie, made from wild blackberries—fresh or frozen—was one of my favorites.

There were many changes in our style of living, as the Irish Foreign Minister had predicted there would be. Some of our visiting city friends were taken aback because our boots tended to track animal dung into the house. Neither Mary nor I could see that it did any harm to our slate floors; it gave the slates a fine patina. We welcomed the piles of dung that accumulated in a corner of the garden and protected them from the rain with plastic sheeting.

We augmented the dung with household wastes and other vegetable matter which we ground and composted. For this we used a gasoline-powered machine called a shredder-grinder which we had shipped from America. Its arrival in Cork City had meant an all-day session of negotiations with the customs people; it was a strange, outlandish machine. With reluctance, a decision telephoned from Dublin Castle allowed the shredder-grinder in without duty, as agricultural machinery. The negotiating process was a pleasant social occasion, this being Ireland.

After that first pile of cow dung we had had hauled in we did not again have to import such fertilizer. Goats, rabbits and ducks contributed manure for the garden. The garden, in turn, helped feed these animals. Our food came both from the garden and from the animals. We had joined a biological network of our own construction.

As we settled in at Dooneen we also became more and more intimately a part of the human community. We did not cut off our relationships with friends in New York, London and elsewhere. Visitors came; one later sent us a subscription to an English-language newspaper published in Europe. We even read it, occasionally.

Our social life more often centered around community gatherings—Sunday Mass and feast days, the annual Kilcrohane Carnival, an occasional amateur theatrical performance, singing sessions at McCarthy's pub—than it did around such things as cocktail parties. Most of our social life consisted of quiet talks with our neighbors. These were learning sessions on many levels, for us. We liked to hear the stories of "long ago." On one occasion, Jeremiah taught me the trick of putting a quartz pebble in the bottom of my pipe, for a cooler, drier smoke.

Mary and I developed our own routine of living. It was no longer necessary to check the newspapers and listen to news bulletins on the radio before we began the day's work, as it had been when we were journalists. We slept a bit later, though we did like to get a weather prediction on the radio in the morning.

In winter, the sun came up late in the northern place where we had made our home. While waiting for its first rays to come over the mountain across the bay we would build a fire in the fireplace and grind the coffee. The mingling odors of burning turf and fresh coffee gave the day a good beginning.

During breakfast we watched the birds feeding on the tray just outside our window. On first coming downstairs Mary piled it with crumbs, peanut butter and sunflower seeds. Sometimes we read a bit, each with a book. We always ended by talking over the tasks of the day.

These tasks invariably began with the animals. Goats, rabbits and ducks had to be fed, watered, their houses kept clean. The goats had to be milked. We awoke at 8 A.M. and left the house at nine-thirty. By 11 A.M. we usually had our animal chores completed.

Next came the garden—planting, weeding, harvesting, roto-vating, then planting again. Each section of the garden was used and re-used in the course of a year, save for permanent crops like berries and asparagus.

As we worked together we planned improvements—a better rabbit house, a better duck house, a new house for the goats, a better system for supporting pea vines. We discussed these schemes over our meals. We often talked of that long-delayed project of keeping bees.

Mary kept quite good records. These did not concern them-selves with costs, but included a perpetual chart of the garden, showing where each crop had been planted and when. This enabled us to rotate crops where indicated. She also recorded each day's yield of goats' milk, with notes on weather condi-tions. When the goats had a good day on the pasture they always gave more milk. Mary's milk-yield book became a record of the weather in Dooneen.

We took our leisure as we found it. If visitors dropped in we left our tasks, to talk. If we had a good book to read we took time out for that. If we were sleepy we had a brief nap after our midday meal.

Because Mary thought it best for the goats we milked them at twelve-hour intervals. This meant working at night. We tried to get to bed by midnight, but more often finished later.

Beginning with that first winter as permanent residents in Dooneen we enjoyed the birds as a major recreational activity. While still using our place in Ireland only for vacations we had concluded, tentatively, that there were more birds in the area in winter than in summer. When we came to live in Dooneen we were able to verify this observation. Our part of Ireland was a winter bird sanctuary because of its climate, mild for northern Europe.

We could not hope to know all of the birds. The mistle thrush we knew and admired for his brave habit of singing into the teeth of a winter gale. The little fox-red wren we knew less intimately because he always seemed to dodge into a hedge as we caught a glimpse of him out of the corner of an eye.

Our favorites were the tits—more often great tits but sometimes coal tits. These handsome little birds are all black and yellow, with the yellow shading into green. Once they were forest birds. As Irish forests receded they adapted themselves to farm and garden. Tits still creep up the side of a stone barn upside down, as if they were hunting for insects on the bark of trees.

Tits were frequent visitors to our bird-feeding tray. Their favorite food was sunflower seed, which Mary arranged to be sent by mail from Cork City. One day I happened to be watching as a tit hopped from the tray onto the windowsill and began hammering with his bill on the window. I called Mary. It was she who understood the message.

"He wants sunflower seeds," she said.

The tray was full of empty sunflower seed husks, which I had mistaken for proper seeds. The tit knew better. Mary put more sunflower seeds on the feeding tray and the pecking at the window ceased. After that whenever the ration of sunflower seeds was exhausted a tit always came to the window and demanded more.

Robins and chaffinches often came to the tray as well, and blackbirds—relations of the American robin, less colorful but

better singers. Occasionally a cheeky mouse would join the birds on the tray.

We watched the bird tray outside the window by the dining table as some watch television. It was live theater, with mouse villains and mistle thrush heroes.

The birds, in addition to their theatrical performances, were always an important part of our garden ecology. Wagtails, pipits, blackbirds and robins followed us about when we worked in the garden. All of the birds helped us keep insect marauding within acceptable limits. Starlings, a nuisance in parts of the United States where they have been introduced artificially, are useful citizens in Ireland, their natural habitat; they are great eaters of insects and slugs.

So long as we kept the strawberry bed covered with nylon netting the birds got no fruit—but the slugs had free reign. As an experiment we took off the netting and found that the total damage was less. The birds ate some strawberries—but they also ate quantities of slugs.

As we came to know the land better we learned to work with the total complex of nature.

Goats Are for Tinkers

Mary and I had known and liked the taste of goats' milk before we had our own goats in Dooneen. Otherwise we would not have made the effort to stock our little farm with goats.

At one time Mary had lived where milk was delivered on the hoof, the goats being driven to the door. Years ago I had visited the late Carl Sandburg, poet and Lincoln biographer, at his farm home on the shores of Lake Michigan. There his wife had kept goats to support the family while Sandburg wrote. It was the only Midwestern American farm I had visited where animals kept for milking commonly leaped to the roofs of the buildings in which they were housed. On Greek islands I had seen large herds of goats being managed by small boys armed only with homemade flutes.

While still living most of the time in New York, but planning for our farm in Ireland, Mary and I visited a goat farm in New Jersey. At that time we also were considering keeping a Kerry cow or two, a small breed that is said to do well on rough land. After visiting the New Jersey goat farm, though, Mary made up her mind in one of those flashes of inspiration that I have learned both to admire and to fear.

"Why anyone would ever want to keep cows instead of goats," said Mary scornfully, "I shall never understand."

Later we invented all sorts of reasons why goats were more practical. The fact was we both liked goats best. Any animals kept to furnish milk were going to require a lot of effort. It seemed better to choose animals for which we could feel real affection.

Mary's idea had been to buy the goats in New Jersey and take them aboard the *New Amsterdam* along with our household goods when we moved to Ireland. I do not, I think, have an excessive sense of my own dignity but the idea of arriving at the port of Cork City and walking down the gangplank leading a couple of goats did not appeal to me.

When, finally, we obtained our first two goats, Fleur and Katrina, in County Down it was a great treat to have goats' milk again. Cows' milk is a poor substitute. In the United States commercial dairies try to make cows' milk seem more like goats' milk by some process called homogenizing that integrates artificially the cream and the milk. Goats' milk comes that way naturally, as does human mothers' milk, which goats' milk rather closely resembles. It is therefore easily digested by human beings. Physicians sometimes prescribe it. We drink it because it tastes good.

There are many prejudices about goats' milk—as there are about goats. If our guests do not know they are drinking goats' milk they think they are drinking just unusually good milk.

If milch goats are housed with billy goats during the rutting season I believe that some odor may adhere to the milk. Mostly, bad-tasting milk of any sort is caused by careless handling.

Any milk unless taken from the animal under clean conditions and then promptly strained and refrigerated will develop an unpleasant taste as the bacteria proliferate.

Neither of us had ever milked goats before, or any other animal for that matter. More of the milk went up my sleeve than into the pail. Mary, on the other hand, seemed to have a knack for it from the beginning. Leaning her head against Fleur's flank she sang to the goat as she milked.

Fleur was a cranky goat, probably because she had been passed around between several goat keepers before we got her, but Mary loved her and the feeling seemed to be reciprocated. Katrina was a gentle and tractable animal, though not yet in milk. She was a bit undersized but beautifully proportioned. Both goats had been disbudded when first born, to prevent the growth of horns. The job had been bungled on Fleur and she had one ugly stub of a horn when we bought her. I worried about this because she often butted Katrina to enforce her own position as Number One Goat.

Our goats became something of a neighborhood attraction. On one occasion an entire class at the Kilcrohane school came to see the goats. Mary served goats' milk and cookies. Later all of the pupils were assigned to write essays on the subject of "Grants' Farm." The goats got a good press.

One of the little boys in the class, Padraic O'Dalaigh—for whom we had named our little cat—later reported to his friends that not only did we have pure white goats but also a silver milking pail. It was not of course silver but it was a fine pail of stainless steel which Mary had bought in New York at a shop selling restaurant supplies. When she first bought it we kept it in the living room of our New York apartment. In Dooneen it was put to good use, not only as a milking pail but for making goats' milk cheese.

Along with some admiration our goats were the objects of derision by a few of our neighbors. "Only tinkers keep goats" was a statement we heard more than once. Tinkers are Irish gypsies.

It is, indeed, difficult to place goats, socially. The patron of the British Goat Society, which also includes Irish members, was Her Majesty Queen Elizabeth II. The Duchess of Devonshire was a vice-president of the Goat Society.

Historically, goats were domesticated—if it can be called that—before cows. As better agricultural methods were developed and scrubby fields were covered with lush, green grass, it was found that cows could produce more milk per acre and were easier to handle. Goats would still do better on rough ground. A goat was called a poor man's cow.

In Ireland this transition from goats to cows had taken place some years before we arrived. Goats had become a symbol of an unhappy past.

Keeping goats was something consciously or unconsciously associated with rule by oppressive landlords and a foreign power. When cows took the place of goats some goats were left to roam in the mountains. They came down to the farms to raid gardens. Hunting parties were organized to kill the wild goats. Only a few farmers still kept a scrub goat, captured in the mountains, to run with cows "for good luck." They gave no milk. They may have cleaned the fields of some weeds which might have poisoned the cows.

Such goats usually were obtained by tinkers in the mountains and sold at cattle fairs. The continued association of goats with tinkers did not help the reputation of either among most farmers. Farmers in Ireland are tolerant of alcoholics, psychopaths—and lone men, "travelers," who move from farm to farm and from pub to pub cadging food and drink. They are not very tolerant of tinkers.

Like the goats they buy and sell, the tinkers are victims of technological change, in part. They were called tinkers because they formerly mended pots and pans, and especially pails.

Plastics have replaced many of these formerly metal utensils. Tinkers sell "antiques" along the road, to tourists. Most Irish farmers believe tinkers live chiefly by stealing.

No one seems to know the origin of Irish tinkers. There are more than seven thousand of them. They travel in caravans or old automobiles like gypsies but they have no racial resemblance to the gypsies of England, continental Europe and America.

Physically, they resemble any other Irish people. They have their own subculture and a language of their own, derived, it is said, from ancient Irish and English. They have Irish names. Some historians believe they broke out of the traditional Irish social system in pre-Christian times.

The Irish Government has tried to house and resettle the tinkers. Priests often preach sermons urging better treatment for tinkers. Though given houses to live in they mostly take to the road again. They remain outcasts.

Our own acquaintance with tinkers began shortly after we acquired our first two goats. One bleak and rainy night a boy and a girl knocked at our door. They were cold and wet, having walked most of the twenty miles from Bantry. We invited them inside to dry by the fire. Mary gave them dinner.

When they told us their names we knew they belonged to a family of tinkers temporarily living in public housing in Bantry. Their purpose in coming, they said, was to sell us a billy goat for our milkers.

We tried to explain that a mountain billy goat would contribute nothing to the milk line of our herd. They had not, fortunately, brought the animal with them. If we had agreed to buy it they would have gone into the mountains and captured a billy goat.

They did not seem unduly disappointed that we didn't want any. We chatted away. They were attractive young people, the girl quite pretty and about eighteen years old. The boy was younger, with lively eyes. It was obvious that they knew little about goats, save as objects of casual commerce. Anyone who wanted to keep goats as a source of milk was, in their view, a bit soft in the head—but they were willing to make a few pence on this as on any other human weakness.

As the night was wearing on and it was still raining I offered to take them back to Bantry in the van. On the way there we stopped at the home of a priest who had befriended tinkers; the girl tinker suggested it. He was not at home.

In Bantry as the young tinkers got out of the van the girl gave me a nice smile.

"We'll come to see you again," she said.

I gave her the price of the goat we didn't want and told her to keep the money—and the goat—and added the ungracious advice that if they were to come to Dooneen again I would only have to drive them back to Bantry once more, a long journey. Her smile did not fade. Her younger brother looked equally pleased.

When I talked to the priest about the young tinkers, the next day, he shook his head sadly. Houses, jobs—nothing seemed to work with that family, he said. One older brother of the pair who visited Dooneen was in the penitentiary on a larceny conviction.

The tinker girl who had smiled so sweetly at me had herself been in trouble with the police on several occasions for prostitution. She also took hard drugs, said the priest.

Our neighbors were sure the tinker family would be back to rob us all. We never saw them again. When the tinker in the penitentiary had served his sentence and was released the whole family was reported to have moved to England. Anyway they left Bantry.

It would, I think, be unfair to leave the impression that all tinker families are like this one. Especially within their own subculture they are said to be at least as honorable as the rest of us. As a people they are handsome. They are horse traders as well as goat traders and make a gay holiday of animal fairs.

If you are an Irish farmer, though, there is no denying that tinkers seem different in some way hard to explain but vaguely threatening. If you are an Irish farmer who keeps cows, goats also are different.

If you look closely into the eyes of a goat you see a strange thing. Instead of being round or even oval, the pupils are oblong, with quite square corners. It is easy to see evil in such eyes and many have done so. The traditional human concept of the devil clearly is based on the figure of a goat, altered by imagination and endowed with unpleasant characteristics quiet alien to goats. No goat I ever knew had the consistency —for good or evil—to make a proper devil.

The Latin word for goat is *caper,* from which our word capricious is derived. Goats are not boring. One never knows what they will do next.

On a fine day when their mountain pasture is bathed in sunshine and the whole world seems a place of joy the goats may become intoxicated with life itself. It has to be seen to be believed that a grown female goat will rise up on her hind legs, then leap off the ground entirely, clicking her hind hooves together in the air like a ballet star.

As it happens, we have a witness to such a performance by Fleur. The witness was none other than Father McSwiney, who succeeded Father Walsh as parish priest of Muintirvara.

It was a fine day indeed when he came to call. In a gesture of camaraderie that dignified man of the cloth, despite his mature years, offered to accompany me as I went to the pasture to bring in the goats.

Before his astounded eyes Fleur danced. The poor man didn't know what to make of it, I am sure.

I was just explaining that St. Patrick himself once herded goats in Ireland when one of the goats gave Father McSwiney a playful nudge from behind that nearly sent him sprawling. Our parish priest was a good sport about it, I must say. He often came to dinner. As it happened he never helped me with the goats again, but we talked of St. Patrick—while sitting quietly by the fire.

Without benefit of clergy, royalty or tinkers, female goats become pregnant, give birth, become ill, recover or die. They may eat too much or too little, behave well or badly. The ancient Romans were right enough when they decided that one who behaved capriciously was goatlike.

One evening we went to the goat house to give Fleur and Katrina a pail of garden-grown carrots each, their favorite feed. Fleur lay in a corner, breathing heavily, not at all interested. Earlier she had eaten very well indeed of the mixed concentrates we were using. We were alarmed at the change.

We had no telephone. The village post office two miles away, from which we usually made our calls, was closed for the night. Fortunately McCarthy's pub was still open and they had a telephone that was on night service through Bantry.

While I, in the pub, consulted the farmers about our problem with Fleur, Mary, in the back hall, telephoned first a Bantry veterinary surgeon, Mr. O'Sullivan, and then the goat breeders in County Down from whom we had purchased Fleur and Katrina. There was not much agreement on diagnosis between the farmers, the vet and the ladies in County Down but all agreed that the treatment suggested by Mr. O'Sullivan could do no harm.

He suggested that we give Fleur a quantity of Paddy Old Irish Whisky, mixed with bread soda and water.

Back home, Fleur was still huddled in her corner. She seemed to be having a chill. Her ears were very cold, a bad sign, everyone had said. We forced the whisky-and-bread-soda down her and stood back to watch.

The change was dramatic. Within minutes Fleur was on her feet and perspiring. Within a few days she was back to normal.

Our own conclusion was that we had overfed Fleur on concentrates—grains and meals we mixed ourselves. From then on, in addition to weighing the milk yield with our dairy scale we also weighed carefully all of the food we gave each goat. One of us supervised the feeding to see that each goat received only what was apportioned her. Fleur's habit of stealing food from Katrina was stopped.

To disarm the bully we contemplated having Fleur's horn removed. We wondered, however, whether to have it done before or after kidding.

Padraic O'Dalaigh, the boy who had accused us of having a silver milking pail, came over one day and we asked his opinion. Having the horn removed before kidding should not interfere with the process of Fleur's giving birth, replied Padraic with great assurance.

"It's from the head ye'd be cutting the horn," he added solemnly.

We saw his point. Nevertheless we waited until after kidding to have the horn removed.

Christmas Candles on the Mountain

⚬ Our first Christmas as permanent residents in Dooneen will always be the time of Job, for Mary and me. Job was the cocker spaniel Mary had fallen in love with in County Down, where we got the goats. My opposition worn down, the goat ladies made the dog a present to us. He was put on an airplane in Belfast and flown to Shannon Airport, where one of our neighbors who worked at Shannon, Finbar McCarthy, picked him up and drove him to Dooneen. A tired, confused, plainly frightened little black-and-white puppy arrived at night. We named him Job because of the sad expression on his face; as it turned out it was we who were required to have the patience of Job.

From the beginning Job was a glutton for love, though he wanted little to do with human beings other than Mary or me. He slept in a box beside our bed at first. Later we transferred his box to the bathroom, which was warmer and avoided Job's disconcerting habit of leaping to the bed whenever we moved. Even as an adult dog he has tried to maintain his

rights to the bed and growls when I put him in the bathroom
for the night. The bedroom is his sanctuary when visitors
come.

Not only did he climb on my lap when he first arrived but
from then on Job followed my footsteps wherever I went,
from one end of the house to the other, and everywhere outdoors. It was as if he knew I had opposed his coming to us
and he was determined to win me over.

In other ways he did not endear himself. I cannot hope to
chronicle all of the crimes of Job. He chewed up the electric

blanket and we gave up that luxury altogether. He then chewed up at least two hand-quilted bedspreads in succession and two couch slipcovers. He destroyed several small rugs. After putting his marks on a fine Donegal rug which had been a valued gift he allowed it to stay in the bedroom. When feeling sick he always went to that rug to vomit. It suffered no permanent damage.

We removed the Persian rugs from the living room. I had purchased them in Beirut and was determined that they not be destroyed.

Job and the ducks became a saga. He would scatter the flock for the sheer joy of watching the panic flight of ducks in every direction. Then he would choose one duck, pounce on its back and take its neck in his jaws. He never drew blood or otherwise seriously injured a duck but the haggard was filled with feathers and down like a snowfall.

On one occasion, though, a duck got her own back. Taking Job unawares, she grasped his truncated tail firmly in her beak. Job took off across the freshly plowed garden, the duck still hanging on and becoming airborne. It resembled a water skier being lifted into the air by holding on to one of those huge kite affairs, while being pulled along by a speedboat.

A feud of serious proportions developed between Job and the postman, Mick Desmond. After being nipped several times Nick took to swinging his mailbag at Job. The only result was that Job attacked with renewed fury.

Padraic, our tomcat, though quite fearless of foxes, badgers, rival toms or any other dog, found Job's charges more than his nerves could stand. He leaped out through the cat flap in the bedroom door in terror, Job at his heels making a fearsome noise that would rout Satan himself. Padraic took to spending more and more time in the Dalys' barn and less time in our house, with Job.

In short, Job was a thorough disaster.

The goats took one look at him out of their odd, square eyes and declared him an implacable enemy. Several times Fleur caught Job with a swift movement of her head and tossed him into the ditch. Job picked himself up undaunted and returned to the attack until I restrained him.

My own reaction to the holocaust named Job did not do me much credit. I pointed out to Mary that although I had opposed getting another dog I had not anticipated such a total burden on our time and energies, not to mention what he was doing to our house furnishings and livestock. I strongly suspected he had been given to us because the ladies of Ballynahinch had found him unmanageable. He was five months old when he came to us and should have shown some signs of adapting to other species, I thought.

I fear that I repeated this theme, with variations, on more than one occasion. The only solution, I added, was to send Job back to County Down.

Mary of course defended Job. He was only a puppy, she said, as if that excused everything. Many times she pointed out Job's obvious devotion to me. Could such love be spurned? I was cornered.

I got a book on dogs from the traveling library and read it from cover to cover. Nothing in the book seemed to apply to Job, who apparently was something outside the experience of dog lovers. Anyway there was a section on training dogs in general.

There followed a frustrating period with Job on a leash while I repeated stupid commands over and over, like "come" or "heel." As long as the leash was there Job obeyed. He did not resent his training periods. When the leash was removed, however, Job continued to behave exactly as before, ignoring commands with magnificent disdain.

Fearful that we would lose our flock of ducks entirely— never mind the eggs (the book said only a quiet, contented flock would lay well)—I attempted to chastise Job with a folded newspaper when he went after the ducks. His response was to run like crazy as soon as he had had his bit of fun with the fowl.

Only Prince, the Dalys' cow dog, was undisturbed by Job. Prince, big for his breed, was several times the size of the cocker puppy. He was tolerant of Job's attacks. Job was, to be sure, playing all the time, even with the ducks and the postman; Prince was the first to understand this. Besides, Prince had thick fur and Job's teeth did no harm.

Only when Job went after Padraic was Prince concerned. He leaped to the cat's rescue, pushing little Job aside with one imperious paw.

More than anything else, Job loved to go with me alone on a ramble over the mountain. On these jaunts he was a different dog. Of course he chased wild rabbits and examined every rock and every flower with his eager nose.

Strangely, though, he had a distinct tendency to follow my suggestions—that he go ahead of me, come back, turn one way or another. He frequently looked at me to see what I wanted. I gave him no real commands; I was weary of that. I simply talked to Job and he responded.

It became clear that whatever his faults—and he had these —he was an extremely intelligent dog. He was, as well, very perceptive and terribly sensitive. He often knew what I was going to do before I had fully made up my mind. If I picked up one gum boot he knew we were going for a walk. If I even looked at the keys to the van he knew it was a ride. He was ready for either.

He was not, to my knowledge, vicious. He nipped Mick Desmond and barked at too many others because for some reason he feared human beings—though not all. He accepted Jeremiah Daly and his son Jerry almost immediately. He was more wary of Kathleen. Indeed, he was more afraid of women than of men, in general—though never of Mary. All I had to say was, "Go to Mary, Job," in a conversational tone of voice, and Job was off.

This did not mean that Mary and I did not feel Job's teeth from time to time—though he never bit anybody or any animal with force. It was as if he understood the English language quite perfectly but could not speak it. His language was to use his teeth. When ecstatic with joy he was particularly dangerous to the seat of one's pants.

You couldn't say he was not full of life—bouncy, buoyant, ebullient, cheerful. He was a gutsy little dog, despite his fears. He never backed away from trouble. In his play-fights with Prince, Job always kept the initiative no matter how hard he was mauled. In our mountain rambles he would climb the highest rocks. He took tumbles but never complained, or failed to try again.

Idiotic as it seems, Mary and I decided to try to reason with Job rather than to give him orders, or if not exactly to reason, at any rate to make clear what we wanted and hope for the best. As he became more and more intimately a part of the family he showed that he wanted to please us. When he did, we praised him. When he continued his wayward habits we showed our displeasure.

We attempted to muster what patience we had. Mary's supply, as always, was better than mine. We did love the little so-and-so. In time I forgot about sending him back to County Down.

It was unfortunate that Job arrived before Christmas. At this season there is much visiting back and forth. As Job announced each visitor he made a value judgment: the tone of his bark reflected his opinion, whether they were potential friends, but not yet; potential enemies; or merely neutral members of that unfortunate species, humanity. His opinions were not always appreciated, especially when accompanied by a mad foray.

Christmas in our southwestern tip of Ireland differs in several ways from the Christmases Mary and I had known in the United States. For one thing, the weather usually is quite mild. There is never any snow. Children do not receive as gifts new sleds, skiis and skates, without which it would not have been a real Christmas for me as a boy in Minnesota.

In Muintirvara Parish Christmas is a religious holiday primarily. Easter, the fulfillment of the life of Christ, is more important than the birth and the promise.

Christmas gifts are exchanged, however. There is a program in Johnnie O'Donovan's hall: a play, music, dancing, all under the direction of the curate. A turkey and a bottle of whisky are raffled. The hall is very crowded and hot with the bodies of men, women and children come to make a night of it.

The pubs are well patronized and there is more singing

than usual. Someone picks out a prospective performer: "It's your turn, Paddy!" Others take up the cry. Paddy hangs back, but finally is persuaded—as everyone knows he will be. "Good man, Paddy!" is the shout that goes up as the performance begins. All know in advance what the song will be, for each of the performers has sung his song many times before, on other occasions. Love and war are the major themes.

Christmas is a time when sons and daughters—and uncles and aunts—return from England, America or sometimes Australia to visit the family. Friends and relations invite the visitors and their hosts over for an evening. They sit around big fireplaces, eating, drinking and talking. Neighbors come in.

The visitors are expected to boast a bit about their successes in a foreign land. A certain amount of decent ambiguity is maintained so that a young man need not explain that his job is cleaning the sewers of London, or a young woman that she is a waitress in a cheap restaurant. Priests and nuns also return to visit their families, some from foreign missions, notably in Latin America. These are the objects of great family pride.

There is a wide gap between the lives all of these visitors are leading "over" and the life they left behind them in Muintirvara Parish. It is not easily bridged. Nothing in the experience of a farmer who has spent all his life in the parish prepares him to understand life in New York, London or in the tropics of northern Brazil.

Christmas visitors who have been away many years are incredulous at the relative prosperity of the parish. They remember dire poverty. They scarcely feel at home in the Muintirvara of today.

There is a tinge of embarrassment to the hearthside gatherings. The fact that Sunday and holiday clothes are worn most of the Christmas season adds to it. The genial, communal spirit helps cover the embarrassment, helps bridge the gaps.

Old men, living alone, stagger home from the pub at night along the long road. No one is left alone on Christmas day. Men and women without families are invited to dinner by friends or distant relations. They will share turkey, ham and the trimmings, the warm fire and the talk.

The beating heart of Christmas, though, probably is best seen on Christmas Eve. Every farm house will have candles in the window so that the Christ child may find His way. You may look up the side of the mountain and see the pinpoints of light dotting the mountainside. It is a testimony to a living faith by the whole community.

Christmas morning at Mass the sermon will be little more than the simple story of the birth of Christ in a manger. Coming out of the Star of the Sea people kneel and pray before the crèche, a cheap, plaster reproduction of the baby Jesus, Joseph, Mary and the animals. Farmers then return home to their own cow barns, to take care of the animals. Only a few generations ago cows were milked in the main room of the house. The doors are still arranged so that each cow in turn could be led in on one side and out on the other. The drain across the middle of the room has been closed over. Still, the birth in a manger seems real enough.

The day after Christmas, St. Stephen's Day, boys dress up as fantastic women, wearing masks. They carry cut branches in which bits of ribbon have been tied. These are supposed to represent wrens.

"The wren, the wren, the king of the birds . . ."

The boys go from house to house chanting in singsong voices, banging tin cans. Householders are expected to give them a few shillings.

No one seems to know what exactly the "wren boys" are supposed to represent. The custom is of pagan origin. Christianity has blurred the memory of the ritual.

One version of the chant by the wren boys—pronounced "ran boys" in the West Cork accent—tells the story of the wren's success. In a contest to see which bird could fly the highest the wren sat on the eagle's back. When the eagle could fly no higher the wren took off and flew higher still.

The wren is said to have been "cute"—a word meaning clever and a bit ruthless. Men who are cute receive a grinning admiration but fail to win real respect.

Mary and I already had spent two Christmases in Dooneen before we moved there permanently. By our first Christmas as permanent residents we were included in most activities, public and private. Mary made Christmas cakes and plum puddings wholesale, the cakes well soaked in poteen, illegal Irish moonshine, as was the custom. She gave these as gifts to friends and neighbors.

Like so many of our neighbors we too had a Christmas guest. She was Marcelle Biagini of the United Nations FAO headquarters in Rome. Although of Italian-Greek origin, born in Alexandria, Egypt, Marcelle found our life and our Irish friends congenial. They, in turn, liked "the woman from Rome."

Marcelle helped us trim our Christmas tree. Few Irish farm families had such trees in their houses. Ours was lighted with hundreds of very small, uncolored electric bulbs. Children came in to admire it. Mary gave each a small gift.

Christmas was a happy time for Mary and me. It somehow sealed our commitment to our new life. We felt ourselves accepted in Muintirvara Parish. We were home.

There was one slight flaw in the holiday season: Marcelle and Job simply did not get on. Every time Marcelle entered a room where Job happened to be the little dog growled at her.

Marcelle wasn't the least bit afraid of Job; I doubt if she is afraid of anything. She was annoyed, however, that any creature should fail to find her adorable. Marcelle is still quite pretty but no longer quite as young as she once was; none of us is.

Marcelle has a rich, multilingual vocabulary. Job was described in graphic terms borrowed from several cultures. Marcelle can be very frank in expressing her feelings.

Job just looked at her and rumbled ominously. It was, I think, a standoff.

A Ham in the Chimney

After Christmas the Irish weather begins seriously to try men's souls. A three-day gale is one thing. A seemingly endless succession of three-day gales is quite another.

Between gales we took the goats to the mountain as often as possible. The pasture was not yet fenced. One of us had to stay with the goats. This would have been necessary anyway because between gales we had what the Irish radio weather reports call "bright spells and showers." By this is meant that anything might happen.

For us it meant not only staying with the goats but also keeping an eye out for dark clouds coming over the mountain from the northwest. We learned more or less to judge which cloud contained hail and wind; as usual, our method of learning was by trial and error. More than once we and the goats were pelted with wet, cold hail—not the hen's egg variety, fortunately; more like sleet, but still unpleasant. We brought the goats back up to their house in the haggard and rubbed them down with towels.

If we were lucky we could huddle by the fire a bit ourselves between showers. More likely, there were other urgent tasks to be done outdoors, securing things against the wind.

We learned never to lay anything down outdoors that was not heavy enough to resist being blown away—and offhand it is difficult to think of anything a gale couldn't shift. Plastic sheeting, paper, spoiled hay or straw, used as mulching, all had to be weighted with stones. Trees and shrubs had to be staked and tied and then re-staked and re-tied.

The fact that the sun might be shining brightly as we worked at these tasks did not mean we could relax our vigilance. The wind would blow and the rain and hail would come pelting down again soon enough. Between showers we also walked the goats to their pasture again. The alternative—and there was no escaping this during gales when there was no respite—was to stall-feed them. This was no easy chore.

For one thing, we had no ready and adequate supply of hay. We picked up a bale here and a bale there. Most farmers put up just enough hay for their own animals. We also needed oats. Fewer and fewer farmers in the area were growing their own. Paddy Spillane, married to Jeremiah's sister, was one of the few and he was generous.

Purposely we had not trimmed the hedges before the gales struck, saving the green trimmings for the goats in bad weather. This meant going out in the wind and wet, climbing precariously on a ladder to cut branches of olearia and escallonia. These we tied in bunches and hung up in the goat house. The animals ate them ravenously, both leaves and the branches themselves.

This fare, in foul weather, was augmented by cabbages and carrots. These items were expensive. They also were hard to find, and farmers who had them usually had left them un-harvested because of their poor quality. We often harvested them ourselves as a part of the price for obtaining them.

At one point during the succession of gales we became quite desperate for hay. We put out a kind of word-of-mouth SOS, talking about our shortage at the pub and after Mass. The response was something that would have occurred in few other communities in the world, I think.

Paddy Spillane gave us four or five bales. Robin Atkins made the hour's drive from Dunmanway, his station wagon loaded with hay. Michael Daly waded across a river to get bales of hay from an old barn where he had a small surplus supply. Finally, one night shortly before midnight John O'Mahony, who both farms and works at the co-operative creamery, arrived with several bales. Most of this hay we were not allowed to pay for. The bales were gifts, based on our own need. All of the givers could have used the hay themselves.

It was on another occasion that John O'Mahony came to dinner and stayed to entertain us with ghost stories, especially the histories of haunted houses in the area. In the co-operative creamery John is all business, inclined to grunts in place of speech, even dour. We were amazed at his storytelling ability, though we should not have been. John, whose place is high on the mountain, has the narrative style of a real West Cork man.

"It was on just such a night," he began, listening to the wind and warming his hands before the fire. This was the story of the priest's house in a nearby parish.

For years one room in the house was kept closed. Few would talk about it. Priests came and went and asked no questions.

Finally a brash young priest was assigned to the parish. He was of course told that the door always had been kept closed but he would not let things stop there. He asked one of the oldest men in the parish why it was so.

" 'Long ago,' the old man said," as John told the story, " 'beggin' your pardon, Father, a priest hanged himself in there.'

"The young priest was very up-to-date like," John continued, "and scowled a dark scowl at that. The whole business smacked of superstition to him; and didn't St. Patrick himself come to Ireland to rid the place of such things, along with snakes and all?"

Forthwith, after returning to his house, the young priest opened the closed door. The next thing he knew he was lying on the floor of the room below, stunned and bruised by the fall. He thought the floor had given away and dumped him through the ceiling but he looked up and saw no damage there.

"At that," said John, "it was not only his bones were shaken. Something strange was up, he knew, but what it was he did not know."

A gale was blowing outside, but no matter. Without stopping for his black greatcoat and black hat the young priest rushed out of the house and into the church to pray.

"As he approached the altar," said John, "whom should he see there, saying Mass, but the old priest who had hanged himself.

"It was a cruel sight. From then on your man didn't last long; he, too, was dead within the week, not by hanging yerra, but by the shakes, which never left him until the grave got him."

A Ham in the Chimney

John knew the story of every haunted house for miles around. Most of them had been lived in by the English or by Irishmen who were believed by their neighbors to have become agents of the English. In the years after John told us about these houses we kept track of the people living in them. They seemed to be a troubled lot, beyond the ordinary human condition.

In one of the haunted houses John had said the ghost was a woman who walked carrying a lighted candle. The people living in that house a few years ago got a priest to exorcise the ghost. He gave it a good try.

"But the priest could manage only to blow out the candle," said John. "The ghost still walked—in the black darkness."

Discouraged, these people moved out and sold the house to some English people. We knew them slightly. Mary asked the wife if she had heard any of the old stories about their house. The Englishwoman scoffed at the idea.

Within a few months, however, a terrible and destructive feud developed between this family and a more-or-less permanent houseguest. Then the husband began running up ruinous debts. Finally the family moved out and left. The house remained vacant a long time.

Mary and I had no ghosts in our house, fortunately. One night a group of neighbors sat around our fire and testified to that. The house had never been haunted.

We did, however, have mice and rats, if not in the house itself—except for the odd mouse that strayed in—then in the haggard and around the outbuildings. Mice were no real problem. I bought some fine little metal traps which worked with cunning efficiency.

Rats, though, as every farmer knows, are a bright bunch of

creatures. I did trap a few. Prince, the Dalys' dog, killed a few. Job, our own dog, chased rats but to my knowledge has never caught one. The persistence of rats the world over is a marvelous thing and one might admire them except that they carry disease and destroy food intended for domestic animals and food for human beings as well. To most human beings rats seem ugly; I suspect this is less an esthetic judgment than a feeling based on fear—fear of their intelligence and their ability to survive and proliferate.

So long as Padraic the cat was about and in good form the rat population in Dooneen appeared to be kept at a bearable minimum. That first winter, however, Padraic apparently stepped into a trap set for a fox. How he got away I don't know. He came limping and bleeding home one morning after being out all night. We cleaned and dressed his wound. The paw seemed to have been broken. It was good news for the rats.

Rats are not indigenous to Ireland. Like snakes, they did not make it from the Continent before Ireland was cut off by the Irish sea. Snakes never did make the crossing. Two varieties of rats proved themselves more cunning than snakes.

Crusaders returning from the Holy Land brought black ship rats to England. The rats quickly found other ships from there to Ireland. Somewhat later brown rats made the passage on timber ships from Norway. I have not seen a black rat in Dooneen although Jeremiah says he has. Brown rats have caused me trouble enough.

One problem is that a trap that will catch a rat also will catch a cat or a dog unless one is very careful. Elaborate constructions which only rats can enter can be put together, all right, but they always seem to signal the rats that a trap is

inside. If a good cat-and-dog-proof spot is found your troubles are not over.

The fact is, rats generally know what is going on. Perhaps they watch slyly from cover. Rats do not much like traps no matter how they are sited.

Farmers know many tricks. One is to put a wet piece of thin paper on the trap's trigger-plate and a pile of grain on the paper. The idea is that the greedy rat, trying to get the grains stuck to the wet paper, will spring the trap. Sometimes they do; more often they don't.

Old rats often seem to move slowly enough to be clubbed by hand. As it turns out, the superior experience of age has enabled them to gauge your own ability to move rapidly with considerable accuracy. They manage to keep just out of range.

There are poisons of course, but again the problem is to protect cats and dogs. It is not easy.

The absence of snakes from Ireland gives rats an unfair advantage. In Midwest America, at any rate, snakes around farmhouses help enormously in keeping down the rats. In Ireland not only are there no snakes but people have killed stoats quite thoughtlessly; stoats are weasel-like creatures and deadly killers of rats and wild rabbits. Hawks and owls, which might have helped against rats, also have been reduced in numbers.

Only after Padraic's paw recovered did our own rat problem become less acute. The battle goes on.

The mother of a Welsh farmer, visiting one of our neighbors, told about a rat getting up her son's trouser leg one night in the barn. At least this has not happened to me—yet.

Meanwhile we had other problems. Our own rabbits seemed to catch cold fairly easily. Some died. They also suffered from ear mites.

Mary became very proficient at administering ear mite powder to the rabbits. At first we took each rabbit into the kitchen. I held the rabbit while Mary administered the medicine. Later she learned to do it without removing the rabbits from their cages. The colds caught by our rabbits, we judged, were the result of bad housing. We put an antibiotic liquid in their water dishes. This did some good, sometimes.

The ducks stayed healthy enough but their social life was

less than idyllic. The drake, ironically named The Com-
mander by Kathleen Daly, took an awful beating from the
ducks when we first brought him into the flock. They went
after him with beaks and wings and he cowed in corners. It
was only after he began vigorously to perform the function
for which we had purchased him, fathering a new generation
of ducks, that he achieved any status at all.

Even when not attacking the drake the ducks fought among
themselves. They divided into cliques. Individual ducks
switched from one clique to another, turncoats. One duck
for a time would be the victim attacked by all the rest, a
scapegoat.

When, later, the new generation came along the social
activity became even more complex. Hatching the eggs was
a joint, harem enterprise. The ducks vied with one another
for fertilized eggs, stealing eggs from nest to nest.

When the eggs were hatched it became a free-for-all to
determine which ducks would get the ducklings to rear. Two
ducks finally shared the rearing of most of the ducklings and
one duck proudly got the rest to herself. The other ducks
became envious, old maid aunts—though for all we knew they
may have themselves laid the eggs from which the ducklings
were hatched. Because of the complexities of duck commu-
nalism the maternity of the ducklings became obscured. The
paternity at any rate was not in doubt. The drake, for all his
initial timidity, was a handsome bird with many fine green,
black and white feathers and great blotches of red about the
face as is the nature of Muscovys.

When not tending their ducklings, fighting, picking slugs
out of the grass or eating the grass itself, the ducks did a lot
of flying. They were an active and colorful bunch. Sometimes

they landed on one of the chimneys at the top of our own house, like jackdaws.

Duck fights and, among the goats the bullying of Katrina by the one-horned Fleur, led us to the reluctant conclusion that other animals are really not very superior to human beings. Aggression plays a large role in the lives of most species, apparently. The power game can be played in the farmyard as well as on Wall Street or in Washington or at the United Nations.

Still, that first winter was not all squabbling ducks and rats running around. Between gales the sun shone.

We had planted a witch hazel in the haggard. Leafless, it developed gay yellow winter blossoms. Jasmine bloomed all winter, and heather. All winter long the meadows were green and the little daisies in the grass kept their flowers. Birds sang.

When we got a radio working we heard reports of heavy snows and cold winter weather in most of Europe. We were grateful for the Gulf Stream.

In a gale we walked to the sea cliffs and watched the waves crashing. Salt spray and sea foam shot high into the air through three blowholes. Our goat pasture was subjected to frequent dousings. Iodine came with the sea spray and the flecks of foam flying. Without iodine goats will die.

We bought a large pig from Jerry Daly and had Thos. Ward kill it. We went to work on the carcass in the kitchen. Pork roasts and other fresh pork cuts we packaged and put directly into the freezer. Hams, shoulders and bacon we salted away in plastic trash bins. Spareribs we barbecued for supper.

Rendering the excess fat, we produced fine white lard, put this in containers and into the freezer. Rendering lard proved to be a messy business, though, splattering the kitchen with hot fat more than a little.

After the hams, shoulders and bacons were well salted we hung them in the chimney for final smoking. In the main fireplace we discovered an iron rod, high up. Years ago all Irish farmers smoked their own meat; now they buy factory-processed hams and bacon. We discovered that the home-made product was superior and that a turf fire, which produces a low, constant heat, is ideal for smoking. The flavor was excellent.

We had had Anthony McCarthy construct a cellar of sorts in a space between the rear of the house and a stone retaining wall. In this we hung the hams, and also would later store root crops and canned preserves. We made a paste to smear over the cloth covering for the hams, following United States Department of Agriculture instructions. Finding chemical ingredients for the paste proved difficult. A visitor from America finally brought what we needed. Insects, rodents and other marauders were kept out by the cloth and its chemical dressing.

Neighbors kept a close watch on this and on our other do-it-yourself enterprises. This was not how they imagined Americans lived. "Long ago," they said, such things were done in rural Ireland, also.

In this period Irish inflation was forcing the price of food rapidly upward. By processing our own lamb and pork we were getting meat at considerably less than half the price charged by Bantry butchers. Similar savings were achieved by buying a whole catch of mackerel and herring from fishermen-farmers, freezing most of the fish and salting some. Smoked salt herring we found particularly delicious. Our greatest savings were in rabbit and duck meat which we produced ourselves. Milk, eggs and cheese we also produced, completing our stores of protein foods, always the most expensive to buy.

Winter was a busy time. Our winter garden produced some of the things we needed. We looked forward to the larger garden, and to spring.

An American Peasant

One day I was returning home from the mountain carrying a bundle of sticks tied with a light chain and thrown over one shoulder. As I walked I smoked my pipe. Job trotted along beside me. In the distance a cow was lowing, perhaps soon to calve. A blackbird sang in the hedge. Job and I were alone on the road.

How had the life we were living changed Mary and me? The question posed itself. Possibly it was only the bundle of sticks and my plodding boots and the small, lonely road ahead, but in that moment it seemed to me that we had become peasants. It was an interesting thought to play with.

Of one kind or another there are more peasants in the world than anyone else. It is still a fact today as it has been since man emerged from the wandering life of hunters and began to practice settled agriculture. Before Plato learned the Greek alphabet men and women working the land, doing the same things Mary and I were doing, made life possible. Behind the knights and ladies of medieval splendor was a great, voiceless chorus—of peasants. They are still there. As a traveling journalist I had seen them in Asia, Africa, Latin America and also in odd corners of Europe such as ours.

What is a peasant? We qualified, it seemed to me, walking along that lonely road from the mountain, because the bundle of sticks I carried were items of necessity, to burn in the fireplace; because the land we tilled fed us; because our animals furnished milk, cheese, eggs and meat which we needed to maintain life and health. We were very small farmers, having but eight acres of land, most of it in rough pasture. Our agricultural operations were diversified; our own labor produced most of what we consumed.

The word peasant seemed important. The dictionary says that the use of the word meaning boor, knave and rascal is obsolete, but this is not really so. In the bourgeois lexicon that meaning persists. Peasants, because of that, do not particularly enjoy being called peasants. One prefers to say that he is a small farmer.

Yet as I applied the word "peasant" to myself I somehow liked the sound of it. The unpleasant meanings are attached to the word by people who really do not know what a peasant is. There is a deep cleavage between the bourgeois of the towns and cities and the mass of humanity on the land. "Peasant," as an epithet of scorn, reflects a deep fear of the great unknown majority of mankind.

A peasant, I would say, is one who loves the earth and works it gently. The gargantuan machines that rape the earth and the sophisticated chemicals that poison it have very little to do with peasants.

A peasant does not own real estate, he works the land, a piece of the earth. A peasant does not work at a job, leave it, and come home to his family. Family life and working life are all intertwined. As New York journalists Mary and I had been two persons engaged in separate tasks. In Dooneen we worked together at the same task. Even what slight specialization there was—I as a plowman, Mary as a milkmaid—frequently broke down under the stress of circumstances. We functioned as interchangeable parts.

The realization that we had become peasants came suddenly but the becoming was a gradual process. One of our visitors from America had been a senior bank official. He was curious to know how we made a living and asked many questions.

"But you have very nearly opted out of the whole money economy," he concluded with something like shocked amazement.

It was true enough that such concepts as price and profit had become only marginal to our lives. To the banker this seemed to be a species of disloyalty to the accepted value system. On various levels many city and town dwellers shared the banker's view. There is, apparently, a widespread bourgeois conviction that striving for success—prestige, wealth and power—is and should be a top-priority human activity. That Mary and I accepted ourselves as peasants appeared as an anomaly, puzzling and probably dangerous. The peasantry is, and always has been, very close to the bottom of the power structure.

Color, speech and many small cultural habits mark the American Negro off from his white, middle-class compatriots. It is the same with peasants, even without the benefit of African ancestry. We might dress in our city clothes but our wind-reddened faces and calloused hands remained as a stigma. On one occasion I made a hurried trip to Bantry, un-shaven and wearing work clothes, and attempted to return a flawed pair of rubber boots to the store where I had purchased them. Disdainfully, the clerk told me that I would have to wash the boots before she would even look at them.

When we adopted the rural Irish habit of having our main meal midday we were not aware of its class significance. It was more convenient. When some of our city Irish friends discovered this fact, however, they became faintly embar-rassed. In their eyes it marked us as peasants.

Being low in the power structure was particularly irritating when dealing with government functionaries. Peasant patience was required.

Our speech did not give us away; when we could not be seen to be peasants we were treated differently. When a house-guest had trouble with the immigration people on entering Ireland I telephoned Dublin, establishing my identity by an American accent and the use of acceptable English. I spoke with middle-class assurance and described our visitor in class terms—as a rich young man, the son of a respected American family. The immigration problem soon vanished.

If I had spoken in a rural West Cork accent, diffidently describing the plight of another small farmer, I doubt if the outcome would have been the same. In fairness I must add that there is less class prejudice against peasantry in Ireland than in most places; it exists everywhere.

Despite the disadvantaged social place of peasants it is an observable fact that small farmers have a stubborn tendency to remain small farmers for as long as they can. History, as Marxists and capitalists agree, is against us. Still, the persist-ence of the peasantry is a remarkable thing.

Those of our city friends who professed to envy us often used two clichés: bucolic and rat race. In this lovely, bucolic existence, they said, you are out of the rat race. What they really meant was that having accepted a position at the bottom of the social pyramid we had no hope of reaching the top and could, therefore, relax. Whether all peasants feel this as an advantage is not altogether clear.

We did live in a setting of scenic beauty unavailable to city people at any price. Our house was spacious and comfortable. Our food was the best. With an 80 per cent cut in our income there were many things which we could not afford; the essentials, largely created by our own hard work, we had in something approaching opulence.

All peasants do not of course live as well, though non-peasants usually are surprised how well they do live. Out of our formerly adequate salaries we had invested in a number of useful little labor-saving machines. We used electricity lavishly. A small pension helped us pay the bill for electricity, our greatest continuing expense.

Our basic security was the same as that enjoyed by peasants everywhere, to one degree or another. The earth fed us. As long as we could work we would be able to eat. The weather in Ireland—though not a few visitors rail at the rain—is as dependably good for agriculture as it is in any place in the world.

To help us remain healthy medical services were available and were relatively inexpensive. If we became poor enough they would be free. If we should be temporarily disabled, through accident or illness, our neighbors would keep the farm going. The life we led contributed to good health. Most of our time was spent out of doors. There was no lack of exercise. We were doing what we wanted to do. We decided when and how it should be done. The animals, whose needs could be imperious, were our only tyrants.

Our peasant security also included membership in a stable society, where behavior was regulated by tradition and custom. The police had little to do. Doors were left unlocked. Bicycles were leaned against a hedge and remained there until the owner was ready to ride again. The sort of casual, mindless crime-in-the-streets that seems to occur in all large cities, was unknown.

"Good enough," our city friends would say, "but don't you miss the intellectual life of the cities?"

The theory that all culture comes from cities is a fiction invented by city people. The only beauty they know is that which they create. Living with the sounds of nature I found myself less hungry for man-made music, though I continued to enjoy the sounds of strings, horns and reeds as well. Our part of Ireland attracted a number of painters, some with fairly wide reputations. I have yet to see any of their paintings equal to the scenery that inspired them.

The art of using words always has done well in Ireland, including rural Ireland. In part this is because the Irish language has been translated directly into English, giving it a fresh idiom and cadence. It was a joy to listen to our neighbors talk, in the pubs or at crossroads encounters. Not only were the forms of expression original but the content was interesting because it dealt with reality.

Many of our neighbors were avid readers. The notion that peasants are "primitives"—unfeeling, uneducated, squalid, lacking esthetic taste—is an invention of urbanites for purposes of self-flattery. Peasant cunning is a phrase; peasant wisdom is a fact.

It is a fact that grows out of lives in intimate communities, close to nature. Mankind is seen in its biological setting. The Irish sense of history is proverbial. A feeling for the continuity of life is a part of wisdom.

So is the ability to enjoy life, minute by minute. Despite our long hours of physical work we learned from our neighbors the value of stopping work—for a cup of tea, talk, or simply to watch a flower or a bird or the way the sea broke over the rocks. It was easy for city people, watching a farmer stop in the middle of some task, to think him lazy: "There's the Irish for you." It is difficult for people whose lives are broken into segments to understand what life can be when it is of one piece.

It was something, though, that Job could understand, walking along beside me on the road. Every now and then he would dart into the underbrush, following a scent, or simply stop and look at something that caught his fancy.

Walking from the mountain, still carrying my bundle of sticks, it seemed to me that I was beginning to understand something important about the lives of people who live on the land, as I shared that life. There was pleasure in it, but the idea of organizing pleasure—now we will have fun—seemed a species of obscenity. The whole of life should be a single experience, with differing modes and tones. And I thought that the peasants of the world, now and in history, probably came as close to this kind of human condition as anyone.

Perhaps this is changing. In many places small peasant

holdings are being merged to create larger agricultural units; simple ways of tilling the land give way to more modern methods. As I thought about this I was grateful that the process moves slowly in Muintirvara Parish.

With luck the changes might be integrated with the best of the past. I thought of Jeremiah's new barn, large and convenient but still homey—a place we often met to fill our pipes and talk. In the corner of the barn was a large iron bar, so heavy it is difficult for a man to use it. "The killer," Jerry called it, but the bar was good for digging postholes or prying out boulders.

Jeremiah had bought it, secondhand, many years ago. No one knows how old it is. Two men can put their weight on that bar to lift a heavy boulder and it will not bend. It is a prized possession and a thing of beauty.

"You don't find bars like that now," said Jeremiah.

When progress sends small farmers to cities and towns tastes become corrupted. Store-bought goods, cheap and gaudy, take the places of cherished tools of sound design. Stable community patterns become broken on the class margin between peasantry and bourgeoisie. Cities grow, crime increases.

It is not, however, the easiest thing in the world to eliminate peasants altogether. A Yugoslav friend had visited us in Dooneen and told us that his Communist country had given up the attempt.

Mary and I had a Russian friend in New York who formerly had been an official in whatever the Department of Agriculture is called in Moscow. One day he was in a railroad train on the long journey from Siberia, where he had been involved in the establishment of large industrialized agricultural operations. Sharing his compartment was a Russian peasant, returning to his old village.

Our friend asked the peasant about his experience in Siberia. The man said he had been treated very well, given a fine house to live in and was paid several times his income in the old village where he had been born. Yet he was returning to the old village.

"Why, then, are you going back?"

The Russian peasant thought for a moment while the official of the Department of Agriculture waited.

"You see," the peasant said at last, "the flowers do not have the same smell in Siberia. For me they do not smell at all—while in my old village the perfume of the flowers fills the air . . ."

It was a fair simplification. Mary and I were beginning to understand it, in Ireland, at the other end of Europe.

Learning to Know Our Neighbors

⚛ If our own calloused hands and wind-reddened faces were a stigma of peasantry among townsmen, among our neighbors in Muintirvara Parish they were proof that we were serious farmers. In a farmyard conversation with a neighbor living a mile or so away he remarked that for Mary and me making a garden and caring for animals must be "a pleasant kind of a hobby, to pass the time away." I answered with some asperity that eating was our hobby and gardening and animal husbandry made it possible for us to eat.

"Donald and Mary work as hard as we do," said Jeremiah.

We were doubly pleased at this. A reputation for working hard on the land was a thing of value. The fact that the Dalys, and then most of our neighbors, called us by our first names— as they did each other—was a sign of acceptance.

We were learning more and more about our neighbors. Their personal lives were as complicated as human experience is everywhere and somewhat more visible. Every courtship, every pregnancy, every family spat was known by the whole community almost immediately. How each family managed to make a living on the land—sometimes augmented by part-time jobs off the farm or by government grants, pensions or by contributions from sons or daughters working in Irish towns and cities or abroad—also was known. All of these things were subjects of endless talk and speculation.

Knowing our neighbors began with discovering the names by which they were called. This in itself was an intricate catechism. It involved not only first and last names but also family relationships and the geographical location of farms.

Many first and last names were duplicated. There were at least four Jeremiah Dalys in the parish. Our next-door neighbor was known as "Jere Dooneen," that is, Jeremiah Daly of Dooneen townland.

John O'Mahony was postmaster in Kilcrohane and also ran a general store, a summer hotel and a large farm. Another John O'Mahony ran the co-operative creamery store in Kilcrohane. The two were confused only by strangers.

John O'Mahony the postmaster was called "John Frank," meaning John, the son of Frank O'Mahony. John O'Mahony at the co-op was called "John Ahileague," meaning John O'Mahony whose farm was located in the townland of Ahileague, up the mountain from Dooneen.

Mrs. James Daly, who lived about a mile from us, was called "Maggie James," using her first name and also her husband's first name. Another Maggie Daly, living several miles further west, was called "Maggie West."

Mary was quicker than I in remembering the names of the townlands and their locations, and who lived where and was related to whom. Our names were sufficient for us. We were the only Grants in the parish. "Donal Dooneen" has a nice sound to it but unfortunately I can't recall anyone calling me that.

One evening we attended a meeting of the growers' co-op in Kilcrohane. We were not members and did not intend to join as this was a commercial enterprise and we were subsistence farmers. We went because we were interested in the problems of farmers raising daffodils, early potatoes and onions for market as well as engaging in dairy and pig farming.

In Ireland the equivalent of the United States Agricultural Extension Service, giving professional advice to farmers, is a system of Agricultural Instructors. We had known one of the instructors in Bantry, Paddy Hanrahan, for he had advised us on some of our own farming problems. A new instructor was present at the growers' co-op meeting, a young man with a beard. Intrigued by the beard, a fashion not then much seen in the parish, we introduced ourselves. The instructor's name turned out to be Tom Keating. He was the son of a prosperous farmer in the Irish Midlands.

Tom adopted the friendly habit of dropping in to see us when he was in the neighborhood. We liked that. Once he brought a pheasant he had shot, Mary cooked it and we all had a good dinner. Another time he brought a pretty, witty and charming girl named Catherine.

As we got to know Tom Keating better we realized that he was a remarkable young man. His education had given him much knowledge of agriculture in its several branches. More importantly, he loved the land and respected the people of Muintirvara Parish who tilled it.

It was Tom's job—and he was doing it exceedingly well— to help small farmers to remain small farmers, but to become more prosperous ones. This was not always easy. Jeremiah, with something over eighty acres of land after selling us the goat pasture, was a large farmer by parish standards. Many farmers were trying to make a living on twenty acres or less.

There were many ways of achieving more intensive use of limited land and Tom seemed to know them all: breeding or feeding pigs, raising chickens or rabbits, horticulture, etc. All of these projects required new skills, which Tom taught. Government grants often helped defray the cost of the capital improvements involved. Tom helped farmers get these grants. He also helped them keep books, so they would know whether their new projects paid off.

One objective of this program was to keep more Irish farm boys at home, breaking the old pattern of migration to London or New York. Another was to provide a paying occupation at home which might be more profitable in the long run than holding part-time jobs off the farm.

A neighbor boy in the next townland, whom I had liked, had left the farm and gone to London. It was a good farm he had left and his father was not able to manage it alone very well. I knew the place; it was beautifully situated, overlooking Dunmanus Bay. The boy wrote home that he was getting a fine salary—working in the sewers of London!

One of the things that Tom Keating taught, along with new farming skills, was that farming, large or small, was an important and dignified occupation yielding great satisfactions and a decent living if done properly. Mary and I believed this as firmly as Tom did. Our neighbors sometimes were surprised that we loved farming and had chosen it in preference to city life. They had been more accustomed to condescension, if not outright contempt, on the part of city people. Tom of course had more influence than we could hope

to have in giving small farmers more confidence in themselves. He was an intelligent and sophisticated young man—
and an Irish farmer himself. He also had the wisdom to speak
softly, with diffidence, in giving advice to farmers.

He was skeptical of many part-time occupations undertaken
off the farm. A farmer who spent much of his time fishing for
mackerel or herring could make some cash income but in
the long run his farm suffered.

There was, however, no absolute answer to the problem of
rural poverty. When there were more sons than farmland some
of the sons had to go. When a man had twenty acres of poor
land and a large family he sometimes had to move fast to
keep ahead of the minimal needs of his children. If that
meant taking a part-time job off the farm one could not
criticize him for that. I had much sympathy for the men
who farmed and did other things as well. I was doing the
same as a part-time farmer and a part-time writer.

In general, though, I am sure Tom was right in saying that
farming is a full-time job, requiring intelligence and concen-
tration to do it well—all the more so if resources are limited.
There is a belief amounting to a superstition among city people that on the farm one can put his feet before the fire and
take it easy in winter. We had not found it like that.

In the winter even doing the chores had an added pressure
because of the limited daylight. As the days shortened before
Christmas there was never quite as much time before dusk
as one had planned for. By midwinter it was 9 A.M. before it
was really light and the light had gone again by 5 P.M. Ireland
is at about the same latitude as Labrador.

On the other hand, daffodils were in bloom by January 24.
Mary and I noted the date, trying to understand the habits of

spring. We were never very successful in this. On many days in January you could sun-bathe in our haggard, but hailstones in April were not unusual.

The ancient Irish Druids held their spring celebrations on February 1. So far as we could tell, this was as good a date as any other. By then we could hear a subtle difference in the birdsongs. Fields, green the year around, seemed a shade brighter.

Every season had its tasks. Before the rabbits in their cages gave birth we had to figure out something to use as nest boxes. Without these, to give the mother rabbits a sense of privacy and protection, the books said they would neglect their young —or even eat them.

Mary had the idea of using plastic nest boxes, thinking they would be easier to clean. The best we could find was a plastic washbasin, so we bought five of these. The rabbits would have none of them. They took the basins in their long front teeth and flipped them over. The notion of using them as nests seemed not to occur to the rabbits.

Finally, after much sketching and some additional research, we figured out a design that seemed likely to please and took it to Don Hunt, who worked in a shop in Bantry that did building and general carpentry. Don built the nests of thin plywood, light but sturdy. They served the rabbits well.

The plastic basins proved invaluable for other purposes. We used them for harvesting crops, to put weeds in as we weeded the garden, to carry small tools, seeds and bits of this and that. To make good use of one's mistakes, we found, was a basic principle of farming as we did it.

Don Hunt helped us with any number of carpentry problems. He made a hay rack for the goat house and a device for holding feed and water pails so that the goats could not spill the stuff. He also built some good bookshelves for our own house.

Don was a muscular, good-looking young man. We liked his ready sense of humor and especially his ability to understand our needs and to help us work out designs of objects in wood. Despite many conversations, mostly about farming and carpentry, Don never bothered to tell us that he was one of the top stars of Irish football.

We learned that, by chance, from a neighbor. Don often appeared on television but we had no TV. We did not read the sports pages.

When I asked Don if he were not the football star everyone was talking about he replied modestly that yes, he did enjoy playing the game occasionally. It was, he added, a young man's game, implying that he was about through with it. Don, as I recall, was twenty-three years old at the time.

"I know a man who still plays, though he is twenty-eight years old," Don added. "Of course," he said, "he is very well preserved."

Somehow I could not bring myself to tell him that I had just passed my sixtieth birthday.

Don's self-confidence was supreme; he could afford to be modest. I liked that. He also taught me a few things about carpentry.

I constructed nest boxes for the ducks myself. The ducks even used them—sometimes—both for laying the casual egg and, later, as places to sit on eggs until they hatched. The ducks, however, also used as nests any odd corner of the duck house and not infrequently a hedge. The neat row of duck nest boxes, though, gave me a satisfactory sense of order, however they might be viewed by the ducks.

Subsistence farming meant jumping from one task to another. Each task brought new problems, and often quite incidental pleasures.

Whenever we worked in the garden, especially if I was using the rotovator, the wagtails came out of the hedges and joined us. They are wholly delightful little birds and quite unlike anything we had known in the United States.

Their name comes from the fact that whenever they move, their tails bob up and down. Most of our wagtails were pied wagtails, black and white, with faces like clowns. Some were white wagtails, a little lighter, and occasionally we saw yellow wagtails. I would have thought the sound of the gasoline motor on the rotovator would have frightened them off, but on the contrary it seemed to be an invitation to follow my footsteps and pick at the worms and grubs, a useful occupation from our viewpoint.

We began planting the new garden plot early in February. It was a rectangle, measuring 130 feet from east to west and eighty-five feet from north to south. Two sides were enclosed by an old stone hedge and two by our new wire fence.

To look at this expanse, which had been plowed and fertilized before Christmas, it seemed a very big garden plot indeed for a two-person family. As we planted, bearing in mind not only our own needs but feed for some of the animals as well, the garden seemed to shrink. At first we laughed at ourselves for having coveted the whole three-acre field of Michael McCarthy's. Later, with peasant greed, we wished that we did have more land.

We planted Home Guard potatoes, an early variety, close to the old stone hedge at the west of the garden, in part to smother the weeds that grew next to the hedge. After rotovating, we dug deep trenches and partly filled them with manure. There were three rows. In one we used cow dung; in one, rabbit droppings; and in the third, goat dung. At harvest time the potato row fertilized with rabbit droppings turned out best.

Goat manure was a close second in producing a good crop. We never had cow dung brought in again. No doubt it is good fertilizer but we had better.

After hilling the potatoes once, we mulched them with old newspapers and plastic sheeting. The mulch kept down the weeds. We had a good crop but there was some greening of potatoes growing close to the surface. Later we were more particular about hilling potatoes, mulch or no mulch.

Our February planting schedule also included Jerusalem artichokes, mustard, beets, radishes, fava beans and sugar peas—the sort one commonly finds in Chinese restaurants in the United States; one eats the pods and all.

Mary developed something I called planting fever. It occurred every spring. Having scheduled the planting week by week she was determined that nothing less than a full gale would prevent us from fulfilling our quota. I accused her of being an overzealous commissar on a Russian collective farm.

Still, it was true that if we got behind in our planting nothing would go right. The giant deep freezer we had brought with us yawned greedily. There was room enough in it for frozen pork, lamb, fish, ducks, rabbits—and all of the vegetables we could grow and process, too.

Also, we were determined to get the best we could from the land we had.

In the seventeenth century an observer was sent out from London to look over the settlement possibilities in the various parts of Ireland. His report from Muintirvara was: "Rocky and frequented only by eagles and birds of prey, never to be inhabited by reason of the rough incommodities." English settlers did not venture out as far as Dooneen, perhaps not realizing that the very winter winds also warmed the place as they blew in from the Gulf Stream.

The Irish farmers had been here all along, working the

land. Mary and I had joined them. We were not convinced that Muintirvara was a place only of "rough incommodities."

"Eagles and birds of prey," incidentally, was a redundancy. The seventeenth-century visitor to Muintirvara was as poor a correspondent as he was an observer.

Birth Is a Tender Struggle

No inconsiderable part of our social life took place inside our little van. There were two front seats. Behind these was a plain metal floor. There were no windows except front and rear. Those riding behind the front seats sprawled or hunched. Several times we managed to transport thirteen people in the van. The atmosphere, to say the least, was intimate.

People owning motor vehicles were expected to pick up those walking along the road. Those without cars simply started walking.

On a routine trip to Bantry we picked up a young man with a beard, long hair and tattered clothing. He said he was a member of a colony of young people and children living in a farmhouse just outside of Bantry. We had heard of them. "The hippies," Bantry people said.

One of the Bantry butchers had talked about them at some length. Immoral they were, he said. Boys and girls living together—and of course children, running around anyhow. Besides, said the butcher, they were vegetarians; they came into his shop only to get scraps for their dog and suet for the wild birds.

The bearded young man we picked up spoke with a soft voice and used good English. We did not immediately recognize his accent but he said he was from Australia. Others in the colony, he said, were from England, America and Canada and one was Irish. They were, he said, Christians. He did not say what sort of Christians they were except that they believed in love. They didn't believe in war or killing of any kind, even killing animals to eat.

This was the first of the hippies we met. Later, many of them visited us in Dooneen. They came to ask about raising goats, ducks and rabbits and about gardening. They were young and talked a lot. Ireland seemed to attract them from all over, especially from England.

What they had in common, in addition to an eccentric style in dress and long hair, was a rejection of middle-class values, though most of them seemed to be of middle-class origin. The Bantry butcher was wrong about their being immoral; on the contrary they seemed to be greatly concerned with morality. Perhaps they defined it differently.

Immorality, in the cities and towns of Ireland, usually means some variation from the prevailing pattern of marital behavior —or from that pattern which in theory prevails. Love, by this theory, is something that concerns married men and women only, and then for the purpose of begetting children.

Love, to the hippies, seemed to be accepted as a normal part of life. It was not our impression that they avoided marriage but they did not insist on it as a necessary basis for morality. They were more concerned by what they considered to be the immorality of exploitation in any form.

This was what they hoped to avoid by coming to Ireland. They were trying to grow their own food. Many also wanted goats, for milk and cheese, and fowl for eggs. Not all were vegetarians.

Not all claimed to be religious, though there was usually a sprinkling of hippies among those attending Mass at the Star of the Sea. It interested me how often the name of St. Francis of Assisi came up in our talks with the hippies.

There may indeed be some similarity between thirteenth-century Italy and twentieth-century rural Ireland. When Mary and I first visited Ireland I had had the feeling that I had been transported backwards into the Victorian era, especially in the cities and towns. As we became a part of rural Ireland my time machine carried me still further back.

The landscape is dotted with relics of hermit-monks who lived alone, or in groups, tilled the earth for a meager living, and devoted themselves to contemplation and prayer—long before St. Francis was born in Assisi. Some of these early Irish hermit-monks predated St. Patrick, it is said. In the scraps of verse they have left they showed much the same feeling for nature as did St. Francis.

St. Francis was, to be sure, a species of hippie himself. He came from a middle-class background, rejected it and embraced a simple life of poverty, peace and love. He also wandered about a great deal and was not altogether well organized; that he was an authentic saint is not because of that denied by conventional Christians. The tattered clothing

St. Francis wore would have blended well with the life-style of any hippie colony in West Cork.

It should not have surprised me, therefore, that when I asked Father McSwiney, the parish priest, what he thought of the hippies, he answered that some of them may indeed be inspired by the Holy Ghost. He was quite serious. Father McSwiney does not joke about such things.

Father McSwiney was in many ways the opposite of his predecessor, Father Walsh. The former parish priest was a man of all seasons, a scholar and historian of some note and also a jolly, well-fed man who always had his pockets full of sweets and small coins, which he distributed to the children as he drove about the parish.

Father McSwiney was thin and austere, at least in appearance. He was a modest man. He often compared himself to Father Walsh and to his own disadvantage. His great love was music and his delight was to play his phonograph at top volume, especially symphonies with lots of brass and tympany. I often wondered what his housekeeper thought of that. Farmers sometimes found him formidable, though one of his first acts as parish priest was to make a formal call at each house in the parish.

When Father McSwiney said Mass it was music to hear. He once told us that he believed quite literally in the miracle of the body and blood of Christ being present in the Eucharist at every Mass. It was a wholly voluntary statement. He was, in his own way, trying to tell us what manner of man he was.

In our many conversations with Father Walsh and Father McSwiney I can't remember that we ever discussed religion at any length. I respected the function of the parish priest in rural Ireland, a position of great responsibility. He is at once shaman, magistrate, teacher and social worker—and often seer and poet as well. The character of the parish priest is of critical importance to the community.

Religion was more important to Mary than to me. To me the great authentic miracle was life itself.

As February waned the agonized bellow of a cow giving birth was heard more often. Not infrequently we saw the Dalys' yard light go on late at night. Sometimes Mary and I went down to watch the birth. Jeremiah and his son Jerry were experts by experience at helping. They knew when to intervene, and how, and when to stand by patiently, with sympathy. They had a gentleness about them. The new calf was brought to its mother's teat quickly. Few calves were lost.

It was the Dalys' practice to wean the calves soon after their first go at the teat. With two fingers and a pail of milk Jeremiah taught the calves to drink from a pail. New calves were kept in the barn in snug cribs made of piled bales of straw, but away from their mothers.

Jeremiah thought that young animals left with their mothers too long would retain the habit of nursing indefinitely. The goat breeders in County Down agreed.

Mary vehemently disagreed. As far as our goat kids were concerned, she believed nature's method was the best. We soon would find out. Fleur and Katrina were very pregnant indeed.

Goats seldom have trouble in giving birth, the books said. Still, the books went on to give various advices concerning

what to do if problems did develop. There were diagrams. Goats, the books said, commonly had two kids, although one, three or four were not too uncommon.

Every day Mary and I went through the anxious business of feeling the sides of the goats for muscular rigidity and for movement by the unborn kids. We listened for faint heart-beats. We watched Fleur and Katrina for variations of habit that would signal an impending birth.

We had on hand more medical supplies for goats than for people—disinfectants, clean old towels, powders, vials and pills. I had become accustomed to seeing cures for goat bloat and scour on the medicine shelf in the bathroom alongside Mary's eyebrow pencil and lipstick and my own shaving things. Most of these medical supplies for goats were never needed.

Katrina was due to kid first. She was an undersized goat and this was her first kidding. It also was the first time Mary or I had had anything to do with a goat giving birth. We were particularly fond of Katrina, a gentle creature—willful at times, but affectionate.

"I couldn't stand it if anything happened to Katrina," Mary kept saying.

One evening, after milking Fleur, Mary spent a long time with Katrina in the goat house. When she came into our own house she announced that Katrina was going into labor. Probably, said Mary, she would give birth sometime during the night—and Mary intended to be with her.

"Fine," I replied, "we'll set the alarm and go down and check things several times during the night."

Mary had other ideas. She fetched a sleeping bag from one of the closets and dragged it out to the goat house. There was a long bench there; occasionally one of the goats slept on top of it, but usually Katrina slept beneath the bench to be out of the way of Fleur's bullying, while Fleur slept on the floor.

Paying not the slightest attention to protests, Mary now proceeded to lay the sleeping bag on the bench. It was there, said Mary, that she would spend the night.

"You go to bed," she said. "I'll call you when Katrina is ready to give birth."

But would I hear Mary calling if I were sound asleep in our second-floor bedroom? I feared not. If Mary could be unreasonable, so could I be. I stretched out on the couch in the living room. Both of us spent the night fully clothed, I in our house, Mary in the goat house.

Several times during the night I got up and went out to see

how things were going. Fine, said Mary, only Katrina, sleeping just under the bench on which Mary was lying, was a powerful snorer. Goats do snore; Katrina had long been an expert. Mary was getting even less sleep than I was.

At breakfast, shortly after dawn, we hoped the coffee would revive us. There were still no kids in the goat house.

By the middle of the forenoon it became obvious even to me that Katrina was in labor quite seriously. She began pawing the bedding, then moved from one corner of the room to another. She lay down, then got up again. Finally the contractions began and the birth-sac ruptured. Mary began timing the operation.

"We'll have to get a vet," she said after half an hour.

We had at that time no telephone. The pub was nearly a mile away; the village, two miles. There was, however, a telephone in a neighbor's house. She was an Englishwoman who was not very cordial about such things, but this seemed no time for details. I rushed over and called a veterinary surgeon only to find that he was not at home and was not expected soon. Then I ran back again to Mary and Katrina.

"Something is showing," said Mary tensely. "I can't see what it is."

We waited. Katrina strained. No progress.

"Try another vet," said Mary.

I ran back to the Englishwoman's house. The second vet's wife said she expected to hear from him shortly and would tell him to come along to us. By the time I reached the goat house again I was fairly winded.

"It's coming," said Mary, "but I think it's only a pair of feet."

Mentally I pictured the diagrams in the goat book, wondering whether we were capable of the major manipulation necessary to correct a faulty presentation. Then I took another look at Katrina.

"Look!" I shouted. "The nose!"

It was, after all, a perfectly normal birth, with the kid's head and front feet coming together. Still, little Katrina was having a hard time. Mary and I each got hold of a front hoof and pulled gently.

When the kid came out Mary was laughing and crying at the same time. Katrina just looked around and began licking the little thing with great vigor. Mary assisted with a towel.

"We'll name it Joy," said Mary, choking down her tears, "because that's the way I feel."

Joy was, indeed, a beautiful little animal. Katrina appeared to agree. Within a few minutes Joy was sucking at Katrina's distended teats. Then she shook herself and began gamboling around the goat house. Once more I telephoned the vet, this time to say that the trip would not be necessary after all.

The next day we took Katrina and Joy to the mountain, where the day-old kid climbed over the rocks like a veteran and began nibbling at the heather and eating the peaty soil close to the roots.

Fleur gave birth to two male kids with no fuss or bother. It was her second kidding. She was a big goat; two kids were nothing at all, she seemed to feel.

After Joy had been born we examined the afterbirth and discovered that Katrina also had had two kids at the beginning of her pregnancy. One fetus had not developed. It was, apparently, nature's way of saving Katrina from what might have been an even more difficult birth.

We were grateful that Katrina had survived and seemed

none the worse for the experience. After a good night's sleep we also might be back to normal.

As for Joy, Mary and I decided to keep her as a permanent member of our herd. We had invested too much of ourselves to let her go.

The two little billy goats, Fleur's kids, were something else. At the County Down goat farm billies usually were "put down"—a coy phrase covering the fact of death—immediately. We could not do that.

We had, for the moment, five goats. When the three kids were through nursing there was even a bit of milk for ourselves.

I told Jeremiah and Kathleen Daly how Mary had spent the night in the goat house. Jeremiah did not laugh.

"Many's the night I've spent in the barn when a cow was calving," he said. "You want to be there to help if they need you."

Life Is for Confronting

"I went to the woods," wrote Henry David Thoreau, "because I wished to live deliberately, to front only the essential facts of life, and see if I could not learn what it had to teach and not, when I came to die, discover that I had not lived."

Many years before coming to Ireland I once found myself alone on a sandy beach outside Singapore. I spent the entire day there, watching the shore birds and the ocean. By the end of that day most of the common preoccupations of human beings seemed trivial.

To say that the insight gained on that occasion led me eventually to Muintirvara Parish would be an exaggeration. It did help me to understand what Thoreau was trying to say— and the even more radical withdrawal from the ordinary affairs of life by St. Francis.

Mary and I had not reasoned out so carefully our own movement from New York, that most synthetic of cities, to rural Ireland, where man and nature lived in such a direct relationship. We made the passage for many reasons. We were not in revolt against anything. We were, I suppose, fairly jaded with trivia.

The South China Sea was calm, the day I spent on the beach outside Singapore. The North Atlantic, when the wind blows, can be a fearsome place.

To stand on the rocky shore on a wild day with the ocean pounding and roaring and the spray flying is profoundly disturbing of the emotional platitudes by which people so often manage to avoid feeling deeply.

It was just such a disturbance, I suppose, that we were seeking, among other things. Retirement seemed a good time "to front only the essential facts of life." There was the wind from the sea, the rain, plants growing, animals being born—and death itself. Death is one of the essential facts of life.

It was still February when Dan Foley's father died. Maurice Foley was a farmer living near Ahakista, a village about five miles east of Kilcrohane. He was eighty-two years old. "He had a great age on him," they said.

In rural Ireland death tends to be expected, and accepted. Dan Foley, though, had been a long time away from home. The death of his father was not easy for him.

Dan Foley was married to Jeremiah Daly's eldest daughter, Mary Frances. As a young man he had gone to England. There he had developed his own building business and prospered. His children spoke with English accents.

We had got to know Dan Foley and his family on their frequent visits to Dooneen. I liked Dan. He reminded me of successful American businessmen I had known. Dan and Mary Frances, though, were moving in the opposite direction from

[174]

Mary and me. Dan never quite understood why we had given up our life as New York journalists to become small farmers in Ireland.

Once I asked him how it seemed when he returned to Dooneen from his busy, urban life in England.

"It seems unreal," he said. "Out of this world."

This made it no easier for Dan when his father died. A traditional wake was held for the old man, however. It was followed by the Mass for the dead. The bell tolled. Dan and his brothers took the coffin on their shoulders and marched out of the church to the waiting hearse. It seemed fitting for the body of Maurice Foley to be carried by his sons. Funeral music, with brass and drums, would have been in order but there was only the tread of feet in the silent church.

The long procession moved to the graveyard beneath an overcast sky. There the old ruined church waited, lending its melancholy dignity to the occasion. Nearby, a field of daffodils was in bloom. In the background the bay was calm. Birds sang.

While the rites were being intoned at the graveside two old men stayed inside the walls of the ruined church. There they argued over their respective rights to be buried in a special place. Their voices carried farther than they intended.

When the volunteer gravediggers covered the coffin they put in the old bones and the bits of rotted coffin from long-past burials first, as is the custom. When the earth was in place and flowers were arranged over the grave the two priests left. All the people then knelt in prayer. Finally each greeted members of the family of the dead, mumbling words of compassion.

From the graveyard the farmers returned to their familiar tasks. The land and the animals still needed them. Only Dan, the urban man, seemed at loose ends.

Dan's brothers were as lonely as he but there were cows to be milked, pigs to be fed. Mary and I went to the mountain pasture, where a crew of men were erecting our fence.

It was a considerable project and an expensive one. To enclose seven Irish acres, zigzagging around rock outcrops, took nearly a mile of fencing. Putting posts on that thin soil was not easy and involved cementing in many places.

We had purchased chain link fencing, five feet tall. Robert Scuse, a farmer living near Glengarriff, and two helpers, James and Finbarr O'Sullivan—unrelated despite the same last names —had been engaged under contract to erect the fence. It attracted a fair amount of attention. Farmers came from miles around to look at it and to inquire about the cost. Many had in mind fencing mountain land for sheep; sheep wire would be less dear than chain link, though expensive enough. For goats, sheep wire is an invitation to climb over.

Not all the visitors were farmers, peasants like ourselves. Our new fence became a sort of dividing line between earth people and town people. The latter had come to our part of Ireland because it seemed to them it was one of the last places in Europe where the countryside was natural and—to use their word—unspoiled. Our fence seemed a species of desecration.

They sent a deputation to see us, these English and American vacation people. We were violating nature with our fence, they said. It marred the horizon.

I could understand their point of view and sympathized with it to some extent although I could see no alternative. Our farmer neighbors did not share my tolerance.

It seemed to them to be an ugly relic of colonialism for slick city people to venture to tell farmers how they should use their land. Our farmer neighbors were happy to see a bit of rough mountain put to good agricultural use. Their only doubts concerned the question of costs, and whether the land in fact would make a good pasture for the goats. Some suggested that we burn it over before putting up the fence. Others wanted us to pour on lime and fertilizer, for which we might have obtained a government grant.

The idea, as one city visitor suggested, that we should allow the goats to roam at will, unfenced, was greeted with derisive anger. It was all too well known that goats, unrestrained, were the natural enemies of gardens.

As far as lime and fertilizer were concerned I was against that, as I was against burning. The things that grew on the mountain that were good for the goats to eat—furze, bracken, bramble and heather—preferred an acid soil. The goats would fertilize the mountain, slowly, naturally. They also would crop the furze and heather so that new growth would come, and would not destroy seeds and the nests of birds, as fire would do. The sight of mountain pastures being burned to promote new growth always saddened me. Whatever good it did in the short run, I felt that in the long run it promoted the barrenness of the rocky heights, once thickly forested.

I rejoiced that the Irish Government was making great efforts to restore the tree covering to the mountains and hills of Ireland. The timber had been cut for the masts of ships, to stoke iron smelters and to destroy cover for anti-colonial guerrilla fighters.

New forests were adding new beauty to Ireland, holding the soil and the soil moisture and providing cover for birds and animals. At the same time I shared with Irish farmers a feeling that Ireland was not just a vacation spot for the rich of Europe and America. Irish land was there to be used by farmers if they could. There was room both for trees and for sheep, cattle—and goats, if the land was used carefully.

When our neighbors saw the new fence go up they viewed Mary and me with a new respect. We no longer appeared as eccentrics, keeping goats as strange pets; they began asking about milk yields. We were able to say that the goats could give more than a gallon of milk a day each and on less feed per gallon of milk than a cow requires. This was impressive.

As the fence went up we got to know the fencing crew—Scuse and the two O'Sullivans—pretty well. They took midday dinner with us. In addition, Mary made them tea and a snack midmorning and again in the afternoon.

Scuse told us about the time he took on a job of trimming

an old yew tree, despite the prejudice against violating such a tree. No one else would take the job, but the yew tree was trimmed without incident.

"The next day, though," added Scuse, "I was working on another tree and fell, breaking three ribs."

While thinking it over in the hospital, recovering from his injuries, he decided to leave yew trees alone after that.

Jeremiah paid the three fencers the top compliment accorded in our parish. They were, he said, "kind." I liked the way the word was used. The best green pasture a farmer owns is called his "kind" field.

During the fencing process we still had to sit with the goats when they were grazing in their mountain pasture. I was nervous about the way the goats watched the fence as the men put it up, as if examining it for defects which they might later exploit. Their eager curiosity was not, in the end, unrewarded.

One day after the fence was in place and the men had left, Mary and I heard a bleating just outside our haggard. There were the two milch goats, Fleur and Katrina, and the female kid, Joy. They had left their pasture by means best known to themselves and come home. We no longer had the two male kids; two of the men who had worked on the fence had wanted them as pets and we had given the male goats away.

We took the three goats back to the pasture and I began what was to be a long process of closing the gaps in the fence. Perhaps inevitably on that rough ground there were many places where the goats could crawl under. There is, I believe, no such thing as a goat-proof fence. At best, a fence makes leaving the pasture something of a nuisance for the goats. What really keeps them in is the fact that they like their pasture and prefer being together there.

Whenever the goats go under the fence, we learned, it is because something has upset the solidarity of the herd. In this first case it was the absence of the two little billy goats we had given away. Fleur was looking for her kids and the other goats followed in the search.

We also learned that giving away animals as pets is not a good practice. One of the young billy goats died mysteriously and the other was allowed to escape to the mountain. We had similar experiences with gift rabbits; usually they ended up mauled by dogs.

Later we sold female goat kids, for a good price, to be reared as milkers. Male kids we had killed for food. When we gave away rabbits for food we killed them ourselves, first, quickly and painlessly.

With the two male kids gone we had a good quantity of milk for ourselves even though Joy was being raised at the teat —or teats. She was taking her milk not only from her own mother, Katrina, but also from Fleur. Joy was a spoiled child. She grew rapidly and was a beauty.

Jeremiah shook his head to see her nursing. She never would give it up, he predicted, and by taking much of her nourishment as milk would fail to develop a healthy rumen for converting foliage into protein.

"Let her nurse," said Mary, and who was I to disagree? We had milk and cheese enough for ourselves.

From New York, Dublin and Bantry, Mary had assembled gear for cheese making—a candy thermometer, the stainless steel milking pail, a cheese press, some old linen curtains. Cheese-making knowledge she had gleaned from several books and pamphlets and from her own memories of watching others do it. Rennet she obtained from a dairy supply house in Dublin; friends brought some Bulgarian yogurt from Cork. For weighting the cheese press she used a variety of things, finally settling on garden stones crammed in a jar.

Cheese making is a complex biological process. The final product could not always be determined in advance without elaborate controls beyond the scope of our kitchen. I cannot remember any failures, though, except in the aging process, when the invasion of molds sometimes was too vigorous. My own preference was for types of cheese requiring little or no aging anyway.

Not only were Mary's cheeses delicious, but they provided a major item in our diet. Fortunately we both were fond of cheese. The product we made from goats' milk was vastly superior to cows' milk cheese purchased at the grocery store— and much less expensive. Furthermore, cheese making proved to be about the only practical way of using our surplus milk. It took about a gallon of milk to make a pound of cheese. We and our guests could consume a lot of cheese. At peak milk seasons Mary made cheese every day.

It was a natural progression from cheese making to another biological process, "wine" making. Gordon Clark, before he died, had given us two books on home wine making—country wines, which is to say, wines made of various fruits and vegetables and herbs, usually not including grapes. To a Frenchman it is a desecration to call by the name of wine anything except fermented grape juice. We were not purists.

Our first batch of wine was made of bee balm, a herb which grew in our haggard and which also is known as the balm of Gilead, in the Bible. Later we also made wine of parsley, parsnips, red currants, furze blossoms, rose petals and several other things.

We began on a small scale, slowly. Wine, even homemade country wine, needs to be aged longer than cheese. Six months is about a minimum.

One Sunday morning we were rushing, as usual, to get ready for Mass, after doing the chores. I was dressing in front of our bedroom closet. After putting on my trousers I picked up one of the shoes which I wore only on Sundays.

As I lifted the shoe I discovered it was full of some liquid which drenched the front of my trousers.

The exclamation which I shouted was, I fear, quite inappropriate to Sunday morning. Job, still a puppy, was into all sorts of mischief and I blamed him for this latest outrage.

When my temper cooled, however, I discovered the truth. We had stored bottles of bee balm wine on the closet shelf. Because the wine had been bottled too soon—before the entire process was complete—gasses had forced out the corks, the wine had spilled out and flowed into my shoes.

This incident taught us a number of things, in addition to teaching me the folly of blaming Job for everything that went wrong. In making that first batch of wine we used a simple method of merely keeping the glass jugs in which it was fermented quite full of water, hopefully to exclude the organism which creates vinegar. The wine had not turned to vinegar, but neither did we have any way of knowing very certainly when the fermentation process was complete.

Later, we purchased ingenious little air locks to control process. Gasses bubbled out through glass or plastic gadgets filled with water, and vinegar organisms were unable to get in. By watching the pressure indicated by these devices it was possible to know how fast process was proceeding and when it had been completed.

By then we had graduated to a series of five-gallon plastic drums. We made a moderate amount of rose petal wine at once, picking the petals from our long rose hedge at the north side of our place, the hedge we had planted while we were still using Dooneen merely as a vacation spot.

As we carried seaweed up over the rocks to fertilize that hedge we had had no idea that we were in the first stages of wine making. When life becomes an organic whole, we were learning, everything that one does seems to contribute to something besides the result immediately intended. It all dovetails.

The web of life—and of death—is there. One does not really escape it, even in a city, though the interrelationships are disguised and hidden—by steel, concrete, conventions and fictions. What Thoreau meant by confronting only the essential facts of life, I suppose, was to see it all plainly and with immediacy, and to become a conscious part of the matrix which we do not anyway escape.

Guests Are Welcome—Sometimes

꙳ With spring came a flood of visitors. It was, so our neighbors assured us, an annual event, like the call of the cuckoo.

At first it was only the casual tourist, strayed off the main road and into our townland, by accident. Some stopped to talk to the natives and were taken aback by our Yankee accents.

I sometimes felt a little guilty at spoiling the illusions of tourists who mistook me for a typical Irish farmer. How would I have felt if, on our first visit to Ireland, the occupants of those picturesque thatched cottages in County Clare had turned out to be New York taxi drivers on a group holiday? The idea, today, is not as fanciful as it sounds. The Irish Tourist Board has constructed "typical Irish cottages" to be rented to tourists; if I were a tourist again in Ireland I probably should rent one myself.

A gulf exists, though, between tourists and the people who live in the place which is the object of tourism. Good manners can do much to bridge the gap. I often wonder if my own

manners as a tourist were as good as those of some of the tourists we see in Dooneen.

Tourists, like every category of the human race, come in some variety. The English have the advantage in Ireland of being accustomed to driving on the left-hand side of the road. It is a little disconcerting to meet a fellow American, driving quite carefully at one, head on, certain he is doing the correct thing by staying to the right-hand side of the road.

As the summer visitors reached flood tide they included Irishmen from abroad, returning to spend their holidays amid the scenes of childhood. A few of these tended to look down on the Irish farmers who had stayed at home. It was an attitude the Irish farmers themselves were quite prepared to deal with.

One Sunday night Mary and I went to McCarthy's pub with Jeremiah and Kathleen Daly. One of the returned Irish was there, a big man with a loud voice and bad manners. Presiding over one large table he developed the familiar theme concerning the wonderful world "over"—a word meaning variously the United States, England, Australia or even Belfast.

No one else in the pub was contributing to the subject. Farmers were talking to each other in quiet voices about farm problems. The women, including Mary, were seated at the side of the room on a bench, discussing household concerns.

Finally the returned Irishman seemed to feel that a gesture was required that would bring home to his supposed audience the validity of his argument that no one who had not gone out into the world of bright lights, dense traffic, air pollution and noise could possibly amount to anything. He turned away from the bar, toward the bench where the women were seated.

"Now, there," he declaimed, pointing directly at Mary, "is a woman who I venture to say has never left this parish in her life!"

With some difficulty Mary managed to avoid smiling. She looked down, shyly.

Nor did a single man or woman in the pub give the game away. Murmurs were heard of "well" or "yerra," that most noncommittal of West Cork expressions. Everyone but the speaker knew that Mary was from New York and had traveled a bit besides.

"And is it really so bad just to stay here in the parish?" someone asked innocently. The man was off again on his favorite theme.

Pubs close early on Sunday night, a fact that one of our neighbors regretted, as we were leaving.

"We could have kept the fun going for hours more," he said, grinning. Visitors to Muintirvara Parish may bring with them more amusement than they realize.

Another class of visitors were those who kept summer houses in the parish. When not themselves using them they sometimes rented them to others. In the spring a parade of strange faces would pass through the village, tweedy English or Americans in fairly violent sports shirts.

John O'Mahony, postmaster of Kilcrohane, operator of the general store and the richest man in the parish, possessed both a first-class education and a good sense of humor. In the presence of summer visitors he sometimes assumed the pose of the genial peasant.

There was a gasoline pump in front of his establishment. One fine spring day I saw two women visitors drive up. John was busy inside the store-cum-post office. The woman in the driver's seat honked her horn and John looked out through the doorway.

"Is there nowhere else in the village where I can buy petrol?" she asked, obviously furious at being kept waiting.

"There is not, ma'am," said John in an even voice.

"Then give me a gallon of petrol," commanded the woman.

"Yes, ma'am," replied John with no change of inflection, "and would you be having an American gallon, ma'am, or an imperial gallon?"

It was as well that the woman could think of no adequate reply, since the gasoline pump was calibrated only in imperial gallons.

One day Mary and I were busy grubbing in the garden when a couple arrived unexpectedly. We did not know them, but it was obvious that they intended to convey the impression of upper-middle-class status. We were supposed to be flattered, I think, by their assumption that Mary and I as former New Yorkers somehow belonged to a station in life not revealed by our present dress and occupation.

Introducing himself, the man got a fatuous smile on his face and extended his hand.

"We are your nearest neighbors," he announced.

At the time we were amused. The couple was staying in a house several miles distant. The statement that they were our nearest neighbors blandly ignored the existence of the many families of Irish farmers living much closer.

Later, when our goats were big with kid, this same man drove his car down our road at much too fast a clip one day when we were leading the goats to their pasture. The goats panicked and leaped into a hedge.

We were not amused. On another occasion the same man's inconsiderate driving frightened Jeremiah's cows along the same road.

Both Jeremiah and we had a few words with this particular visitor. His excursions in Dooneen became infrequent.

Many friends and relations came to Dooneen to see Mary

and me, beginning within a week or so of our move there. We had the converted barn in which to house them. Such visits lasted from a day or two to several weeks.

We tended to be rather free with invitations. We wanted to share the pleasure of our new life. Some guests arrived without being invited; they had heard of us, back in America, and were passing this way.

Several problems arose. It was not easy to convey to our guests the fact that we were very poor. That we produced much of our own food did not mean that it was free. Our supply of labor, as well as of money, was limited. Land, tools, electricity, feed for the animals, were all considerable items of expenditure.

Some friends who had known us in New York could not seem to be undeceived of the notion that we were on some kind of a lark—a perpetual house party. I tried to bring them back to reality by pointing out—usually in letters replying to suggestions that they would like to come for a visit—that we kept no whisky in the house, and that guests were expected to work, as we did. These ungracious warnings did not discourage many from coming.

We tried to assign compatible tasks to our guests. One couple came without bringing any work clothes and our own spare gear did not suit them. Mary got the idea that anyway they could pick wild blackberries along the country lanes.

"How unfortunate," replied the male of this pair, "that I have not brought with me a pair of glasses suitable for such work." He spent his time reading, in the guesthouse. He also was unable to build a fire there, so I did it. This incident was not altogether exceptional.

A few guests, however, worked very hard and more than earned their keep. Among these were a number of students, one author of books on international politics, an official of the British Information Service in New York and a Greek scholar who also was an accomplished pianist.

Mary and I discovered that friends we had known for many years, elsewhere, appeared in quite a different light when they visited us in Dooneen. Qualities which were amusing in New York were, I fear, sometimes less so when the task at hand was cleaning the goat house.

In time we learned not to expect too much from our guests in the way of work. The most important quality in a good guest we found was sensitivity: the ability to appreciate man and nature in a strange setting. A sensitive person also was able to feel when an hour of witty and charming conversation would be acceptable—and when pitching in quietly at the task at hand was more to be desired.

We were somewhat surprised, though perhaps we should not have been, that very young guests seemed to fit in best. We still talk fondly of a fifteen-year-old American girl and a twelve-year-old English boy who, separately, each found Dooneen a place to love and to be loved. The animals pined for them when they left. A few adults achieved the same rapport. At the other end of the scale were the fastidious people who carefully walked around animal droppings.

Mary was considerably more gracious to our guests, both in inviting them and while they were in Dooneen, than I was. I sometimes retreated into the garden or to the goat pasture. My idea of a good friend was a fellow farmer who would stop and smoke his pipe and chat for a while in the haggard, but who had as many chores waiting for him, and much the same sort of chores, as I did.

As a peasant I fear I was sometimes the grumbling sort. This did not mean that I failed to enjoy life, with or without guests. Mary's disposition is happy enough for both of us. I sometimes found it difficult to work the land and take care of the animals and at the same time to be the perfect host. Still, our guests did bring with them the flavor of the world "out there." As each guest, or batch of guests, departed, Mary and I found ourselves more satisfied than ever with our life in Dooneen.

One spring visitor we all welcomed was the cuckoo. Spring was not official until he came. Working in the garden, Mary and I heard the cuckoos calling from the trees around the three-thousand-year-old earthworks on the edge of the cliff and an answering call from a clump of trees up towards McCarthy's barn. As the cuckoos flew back and forth they gave their cry on the wing.

It is not a lovely sound and some grow weary of it quickly. Mary and I, who, before we came to Ireland, had known the song of the cuckoo only by listening to cuckoo clocks—which do manage to reproduce nature very well—found the original sound both amusing and exotic.

We knew, too, that cuckoos eat quantities of hairy caterpillars which other birds avoid. Any creature that helped get rid of garden pests was doubly welcome.

That cuckoos lay their eggs in the nests of other birds is well known. They are not alone in this habit, shared by some eighty species. It is, to be sure, a regrettable form of exploitation, especially when the cuckoo invades the nest of the gentle meadow pipit, steals an egg, replaces it with one of her own— and then calmly eats the stolen egg.

More remarkable is the migration of the cuckoo. Bird migration in general is difficult enough to understand. The cuckoo is a special case.

The hatched cuckoo never knows its parents and may have no communication at all with other members of its species before migration. Nevertheless, when the time comes, the cuckoo takes off from Ireland and flies to Africa for the winter and there joins a colony of cuckoos each member of which has performed a similar feat.

Somehow implanted in the egg is not only the impulse to migrate—but instructions as to the destination, and how to get there. Talk about genes and instincts begs the question and the fundamental mystery remains. The navigator on an airplane, surrounded by a clutter of electronic devices and himself elaborately educated in his job, using maps, fixing his course by the stars, may have difficulty guiding his plane from Ireland to Africa. It is all there in the little egg of the cuckoo when it is laid in the nest of the meadow pipit, the dunnock or the robin.

Not waiting for the cuckoo to make spring official Mary and I already had planted asparagus. This was a major job and we did it as well as we could, for once asparagus is well laid down, the bed, with proper care, will yield for twenty years or more. We dug two trenches, eighteen inches wide and the same depth. In these we put a good quantity of goat dung. Because the dung was mixed with moss peat we had used as bedding for the goats we also added lime. We then shoveled in some earth and formed this into ridges in the center of each trench.

We were now ready for the asparagus crowns. We had arranged to get these from Michael Daly, a farmer living near the village. Mary and I dug the plants ourselves and hurried home with them in the van so they could be planted before they dried out. Carefully we placed the crowns in the trenches so that their roots spread out and down from the ridges. We then covered the lot with earth and sprinkled on a little more lime.

In the process of getting the asparagus crowns we came to know the Michael Daly family better. This was by far our greatest gain in the transaction.

Michael was an Irishman who had left Ireland, wandered around the world, then returned to the life he had discovered was the best. He once told me he had held forty different sorts of jobs—and that farming was the most interesting and demanding of them all.

Ann Daly, his wife, was the daughter of the blacksmith of Kilcrohane. She was the mother of six children and often worked in the fields with Michael as well as taking care of the house and the family. Despite this she had retained her figure and good looks. She could have passed for an unusually pretty college girl. Ann and Michael were intelligent, well informed, and possessed a lively sense of humor and a capacity for enjoyment.

The Daly children were a joy to know. The eldest was ten years old. All were beautiful and full of life.

In getting seaweed to fertilize the asparagus bed we also became better acquainted with two very young men from Kilcrohane—Jim Tobin and Dermot Daly, the latter no relation to Michael. With a tractor and trailer they gathered the seaweed and hauled it to us. We needed more than we could hope to bring up over the rocks of Dooneen ourselves. After the seaweed was delivered Jim and Dermot stayed for tea.

This was the occasion for much bantering conversation. Mary teased the boys about the girls. Both were handsome, but like all young men in rural Ireland, reticent on this subject. They blushed.

They preferred to talk about Jim's goat. The goat, a scrub animal Jim had captured in the mountains to follow his cows, was a familiar sight on the village streets.

She also grazed in the churchyard and was not above entering the Star of the Sea on occasion.

"One thing," said Jim, "when the goat entered the church she didn't misbehave."

The sexton, not noted for his sense of humor, found Jim's goat a trial. On one occasion the goat entered the church during services. The sexton evicted her, threatening the animal with his candlesnuffer. There was much suppressed laughter in which the sexton did not join.

Finally one day the Bishop of Cork came to inspect the church, newly decorated. As he walked up the aisle, attended by the parish priest and the curate, who should be following but Jim's goat.

The curate had some harsh words to say about that, but as Jim told us, grinning, what can you do about a goat?

One thing Jim did was to get her bred. To do this he went to the mountain again and this time captured a billy goat, a nimble accomplishment. Two male kids were born, increasing the sexton's worries by that much.

In the process of spreading the seaweed that Jim and Dermot brought for our asparagus bed I discovered a great collection of foreign matter which had been dumped in the sea and had washed up on the beach where the seaweed was gathered. Included in the collection were ugly lumps of solidified oil, the residue of the stuff that came from tankers when they were washed out at sea. Also included were many bits of plastic—parts of deck covering, engine tubing, oil cans, and a pair of spectacles, minus lenses.

Irrationally, perhaps, it angered me to find this stuff in the seaweed. Green fields all around us testified to the fact that seaweed had been used as fertilizer for a thousand years. How much longer it would be fit to use was a question.

Plastic in the seaweed and tourists on the road were warnings that the processes and values of the cities from which we had fled were following on our heels. It was not a pleasant thought.

When I told John O'Mahony, the postmaster, about the foreign matter in the seaweed he had a comment.

"Pollution," he said. "And people are the greatest pollution of all."

An Irish Policeman—in Ireland

Mary and I came to Ireland as aliens and remained so. There were several reasons for this. We were Americans by birth, culture and tradition. It would have been foolish to pretend to others or to ourselves that we had somehow become Irish. Our position would not have been improved.

To be an American is not to be totally foreign in rural Ireland. I cannot recall any of our neighbors who did not have relations living in the United States. Whatever our legal status, to them we would always be "the Yanks," as were their own cousins in Casper, Wyoming, where many emigrants from the parish had gone as ranchers.

It was important, we felt, to keep our own identities unconfused. We preferred to avoid the role of American expatriots in such places as Paris, Rome and Mexico City. The more they tried to maintain their own feelings of being Americans, by creating little ghettos, the more they became strangers—to the people of the countries where they were living and to themselves, without in the process avoiding alienation from the United States as well.

We did not seek out our fellow Americans in Ireland and saw them infrequently. Our closest friends were our Irish neighbors. That they accepted us as Americans helped us accept ourselves as we were.

There were advantages in remaining frankly foreigners though living permanently in Ireland. Our Irish neighbors were, I think, more tolerant when we departed from local customs; we were subjected to fewer taboos. When we chose to conform, on the other hand, this was appreciated precisely because we were not Irish.

"Ye are like ourselves" became a cherished comment, no matter how frequently made.

As foreigners intending to be permanent residents in Ireland we had to register with the police. This, as it turned out, was no small undertaking.

The nearest police station was at Durrus, twelve miles to the east of Dooneen. Durrus also had been the nearest seat of the old Irish Ascendancy, that odd collection of pretentious power that presided over Ireland when the British ruled the island. Something of the old flavor remained, like the odor of stale beer in a pub long abandoned. That the police station was in Durrus was an unfortunate reminder that the gardai was the successor to the Royal Irish Constabulary, the Ascendancy's police force. For this reason a policeman's lot in Ireland was still not a particularly happy one. Most Irish policemen, we had found, were almost excessively polite, but ordinary Irish farmers still did not completely trust the gardai.

When we drove to Durrus to register with the police we found the officer in charge bent over his desk, deep in a profusion of papers. We explained our errand. He looked at us with an expression of pain.

"Could ye possibly postpone your registration for a week or two?" he asked.

A little annoyed, I explained that we were trying to abide by Irish regulations. We had, I added, made the trip to Durrus especially to register with the police.

"That I understand," he said, "but, you see, I have been transferred from this parish. Just now I am up to here in paper work, getting ready to turn over to the man who replaces me. It would be a great convenience to me if you would wait and register with him. Otherwise I shall have even more paper work to do."

We drove back home, feeling that whatever else living as aliens in Ireland might mean it did not require a very strict adherence to rules and regulations. We were wrong about that. We had not counted on Sergeant Moran.

He was the new police officer in Durrus. When we got around to driving there again Sergeant Moran greeted us with a stony eye.

We explained ourselves, pointing out that we had tried to register previously as we did not want to neglect this requirement. Sergeant Moran silently opened a book of regulations. For a few minutes he read in silence.

"I see," he said at length. "I see."

He then began an inquisition that would have been adequate had we been drug smugglers or importers of cattle suffering from hoof-and-mouth disease. There were no snags, though, until he came to the question: "What is your permanent residence?"

"Dooneen," Mary answered happily.

Sergeant Moran looked up from his desk.

"I mean, in America," he said.

"But of course we have no permanent address in America," Mary replied. "We gave up our apartment in New York and moved to Dooneen."

"Lock, stock and barrel," I added unoriginally.

Sergeant Moran considered this. "But where were you born?" he asked.

I explained that Mary had been born in West Virginia and I in Minnesota.

"Yes," he said, "and what is your permanent address, then?" We were right back where we started.

Mary at this point was beginning to lose her usual good humor. This was apparent to me and also, it seemed, to the sergeant. He made a strategic retreat to regroup his forces.

"I will send in a report to Dublin Castle," he said. "They will have to decide."

Again we left the police station in Durrus, still not quite registered as permanent alien residents.

A day or so later Sergeant Moran appeared in person at Dooneen. The tone of the conversation went a little better, over a cup of coffee before the fire, but the content was much the same as before.

"There is no use asking again where our permanent home is," said Mary at length, "for you are in it."

Still unsmiling, still very polite, Sergeant Moran left. What Dublin Castle would do about us, he said, was hard to know. . . . No doubt we would be required to report to the police every few months. . . . That was the regulation . . .

As it turned out we were required to do no such thing.

Dublin Castle sent our certificates of registration with a notation that we would be "permitted to reside in this country
. . . without condition as to time."

I hadn't the heart to complain to Sergeant Moran that by
some clerical error my name had been changed on the registration certificate from plain Donald Grant to Donald Smith-
Grant. My middle name, as shown on my American passport,
was indeed Smith—my mother's maiden name—but I never
used it. To this day I suppose I am listed in the Dublin Castle
police files under *S* rather than *G.*

Sergeant Moran was impressed: not by the hyphen, I trust,
but by the fact that Mary and I had been given status as permanent residents without qualification and need not even report periodically to the Durrus police station. This did not,
however, end our connection with Sergeant Moran. From
then on whenever he was out Dooneen way he usually
stopped in for a cup of coffee. He was, we found, a decent,
friendly man for all the awkward silences that punctuated his
conversation. It was, we concluded, a style not adopted by
accident.

Since Irish farmers were not very frank with police officers,
Sergeant Moran apparently hoped that we, as foreigners con-
versant with local gossip, would be more useful. The silences
were there for us to fill in if we chose to do so. We adopted a
tactic, in this situation, of filling the gaps with all sorts of information that would not be very useful to the sergeant—how
the crops were growing, who had given birth to a baby, who
was about to be married and the price of pigs.

With elaborate unconcern, Sergeant Moran began dropping
the name of Healy. There was no one named Healy in our

neighborhood and this puzzled us at first. Often the name of Healy was followed, after a suitable interval, by the equally casual mention of the Dooneen pier.

Sergeant Moran was the last man to explain what this was all about. Our neighbors were somewhat more informative. Slowly we pieced the story together.

The man named Healy actually did exist. He had arrived one day on the Bantry Bay side of the mountain, purchased or rented a bit of land and installed on it two large and obviously expensive house trailers. With Healy had come his wife and a child and a second man, also apparently with wife. This explained the two house trailers well enough.

Around the trailers were accumulated a number of vehicles. These included an ordinary passenger car, a Land Rover—and an enormous amphibious creature, obviously left over from World War II. When it moved on the road it left room for nothing else. What it did in the water we never witnessed.

Despite his Irish name, Healy had an English accent. Shortly after he arrived—and long before Sergeant Moran began mentioning the name of Healy to us—an event had occurred that brought the name of Healy high on the list of topics for pub talk. Mary and I had missed it because at the time we were involved in one of the many farming crises that arose from time to time on our own place.

In the gray hours just before dawn, it seems, a formidable crowd of police, including representatives of Scotland Yard in London, had descended on Healy's little caravan community. The police were armed with search warrants. What they were looking for, no one seemed to know, but they found nothing and retired in some embarrassment.

At the time Sergeant Moran started visiting us apparently he hoped to retrieve the situation, so far as the police were concerned, by discovering through indirect methods what had eluded discovery through a pre-dawn raid. Healy was a man of mystery and Sergeant Moran was determined to solve this case if it took unlimited hours of Mary's and my time and no small quantity of Bewley's coffee, imported from Dublin.

Sergeant Moran's mention of Dooneen pier fitted into the mystery because, so our neighbors said, Healy and friends were making frequent trips down our small lane to the pier, where they had a boat and sometimes two boats riding at anchor. Fishermen had seen the men load into their boats a quantity of equipment used for deep diving.

The pier we knew. It is an impressive stone structure reportedly built as made-work around the turn of the century. It has no very serious function although a few fishermen use it. It is large enough for a battleship to be anchored alongside it and a bollard on a rock outcrop in the bay beyond the pier seems to have been constructed to help hold in place just such a vessel.

No one remembers a warship ever having been tied to the pier. Mary, however, once dove into the bay from the pier only to scramble out again at the approach of a small army of sting rays. We also had caught a few crabs there, in a lobster pot, and had hooked a fish or two.

For the first time in its long history Dooneen pier now became the focus of serious official attention. From time to time we could hear motor vehicles pass on our lane, on the way to the pier, and heard them return again. Our view of the lane is obscured by hedges.

Sometimes, though, we were able to make out that the

passing vehicle was driven by a man with a beard. At other times the driver seemed to be wearing a police uniform. General curiosity was much whetted.

One day Healy himself, the man with the beard, stopped by our place, presumably to ask about the possibility of buying a goat. This was no more his real purpose than Sergeant Moran's purpose was drinking coffee. Healy seemed as anxious to know about Sergeant Moran as Sergeant Moran obviously was eager to know about Healy. Healy, though, was the more ready talker of the two. He was full of lively chatter—without revealing anything of his purpose in visiting Dooneen pier, or for that matter his purpose in being in Ireland at all.

Fishermen from whom we purchased Dunmanus Bay mackerel and herring, proved in the end to be our best sources of information. Three Castle Head, across the bay, was a notorious ship graveyard. For centuries ships had struck rocks there and gone to the bottom. One historian of such things estimated that there were several hundred ships on the bottom off Three Castle Head. Fishermen were convinced that Healy and his friends, with their diving equipment, were engaged in looking for sunken treasure aboard the wreckages at the bottom of the sea.

Healy's furtive actions, the fishermen thought, could be explained by the fact that under Irish law the government would take a large slice of any treasure found, if it was reported. In the fishermen's view Healy was more than justified in avoiding such payments.

"If a man has the nerve to dive to the bottom of the sea," one of the fishermen told us, "I don't care whether he is English or Irish or what he is—what he finds should be his to keep."

What, if anything, Healy found was never known. The story was that he injured his lungs diving and became desperately ill. In any event the Healy caravan eventually disappeared from our peninsula and the whole episode became a part of the folklore of Muintirvara Parish.

It had afforded us some opportunity for knowing Sergeant Moran a little better. I had begun my newspaper career as a police reporter during the Prohibition era in the United States. The Healy episode stirred old memories.

Sergeant Moran, it should be added, proved himself a good police officer on a later occasion when thieves entered the home of an Englishwoman living near us, while the woman was gone. By clever sleuthing, Sergeant Moran not only found out who committed this crime but recovered the stolen goods and sent the man to prison, convicted of larceny.

This successful police work was welcomed in our neighborhood because the criminal turned out to be no one living in the parish, but a tinker, a "traveler," from far away. We could still trust each other in the parish and continue to be fairly careless about locking doors.

The good sergeant seemed to relax somewhat after this success. He was even seen to smile. Later, when, after having been married for a number of childless years, his wife gave birth to a son, Sergeant Moran became positively human.

During this period there was much trouble in Northern Ireland. The Irish Republican Army, illegal both in the North and in the Republic, was much involved. It was generally believed that arms for the IRA were being smuggled into the Republic from precisely such places as Dooneen pier. It is interesting that no one talked very much about this possibility at the time of the Healy episode. If IRA arms were coming ashore at Dooneen no one wanted to know about it, with the exception of Sergeant Moran.

He was a thoroughly conscientious police officer. The face of the law in Ireland, in the person of the good sergeant, was friendly and fair-minded but unrelenting toward possible violations of the law of any sort. He once asked if Job had a dog license. Another time he mentioned that our registration sticker on the van was near to the date of expiration.

On one occasion Sergeant Moran obviously thought he had caught Mary and me in a most flagrant situation, though it was equally obvious that the exact nature of that situation eluded him. The American Museum of Natural History had recorded the howling of wolves in Canada and Alaska. One of Mary's uncles had sent us the recording.

We were playing it at considerable volume on the phonograph when Sergeant Moran happened to drop in. I shall never forget the look on his face as he entered our house— warily looking this way and that for the pack of wolves.

We turned off the phonograph and Mary brewed fresh coffee. Sergeant Moran's visits became somewhat less frequent after that.

Lords and Ladies Are After Going

⊰ On a fine spring day in Dooneen it is difficult to think of the disadvantages of living in rural Ireland, but they exist. Mary and I frequently were approached by other Americans who were considering Ireland as the place for a new, permanent home. Usually these requests came from people contemplating retirement, or young people, dissatisfied with urban life in the United States and seeking a new kind of existence.

Ireland, we told them, is not for everyone. It is a place of bright spells and showers, to use the phrase which occurs most often in weather predictions over the Irish radio. One had better take good advantage of the bright spells and not mind the showers too much. This goes for more than the weather.

When our mounting farm chores permitted, and sometimes incidental to them, Mary and I walked by the sea in the spring sunshine. Job went with us on errands of his own. On such days it was impossible to take any problem too seriously. We enjoyed the sun and air and the wild flowers, creamy yel-

low primroses, deep blue violets and sea pinks. In a sandy place close to the sea we discovered a little colony of burnet roses. Furze blossoms covered the mountains and moorland; ours was a golden landscape.

We started a hare in a pine grove as we passed. On the lane ahead a bushy-tailed fox turned to stare at us for an instant before he disappeared into the brush with deceptive deliberation.

Hare and fox were delicious odors to Job, a trail to follow. It was a game that harmed no creature and gave him much pleasure.

At the close of the day the full-throated song of the blackbird was joined by the spectacular elaborations of the song thrush. The blackbird was in the hedge, the song thrush in a treetop. Together they were an orchestra.

Mountains loomed behind us. There were other mountains across the bay. At the mouth of the bay was the endless vista of the open Atlantic. The sky was blue, with billowing white clouds.

This was our home.

Taking it all in with a sigh, Mary remarked for the hundredth or five-hundredth time how lucky we were to be able to live in such a place, and for the rest of our lives. It was not a brief interlude, after which we must return to cities and grime, to worry and strain. It was life itself, our own new life.

And yet . . . and yet, before we attempted to advise others who hoped to duplicate our happiness by themselves moving to rural Ireland we sat down in the cool of evening to construct a catalogue of problems and disadvantages the average American would have to face. We had faced them ourselves.

Such a list might well start with rain and rheumatism. Some people become depressed when it is raining. They had better retire to Arizona. Without bothering with average annual rainfall figures it is clear that it does rain in Ireland.

Mary and I were in disagreement as to the effect of damp weather on arthritis or rheumatism. It seemed to me that one's joints ached more on a damp day. Mary had all sorts of scientific reasons for claiming that the climate made no difference.

Certainly central heating makes damp weather easier to bear. On the other hand, we spent most of our time, rain or shine, out of doors. In honesty, we were not entirely free of ailments attributed by our good Irish doctor, Jerry Murphy, to arthritis. It did not interfere with our work, or with our happiness.

Although we had come to Ireland in preference to southern Italy or Greece, in part because the cultural differences were fewer for Americans, it would be folly to ignore the differences that do exist. They are several, and sometimes take unexpected forms.

In our parish little or no Irish was spoken. Children were forced to learn some Irish in school but most of them quickly forgot it. English was spoken universally—but the West Cork accent was something else.

One of our houseguests was a former associate of Mary's in New York, a girl of Irish extraction but thoroughly Americanized. On the way to Dooneen she had taken a sight-seeing bus trip, with frequent stops. When she arrived in Dooneen she described the trip.

"Our family tradition," she said, "was that our ancestors spoke the Irish language entirely, but I had thought it was not widely spoken any more. I was surprised that almost everyone, especially in West Cork, speaks Irish all the time."

Mary and I were even more surprised, but said nothing. Later, we introduced our guest to Jeremiah Daly, who welcomed her to Dooneen and made a few remarks about the weather. When we had returned to our house our guest from New York turned to Mary.

"Could you understand what Mr. Daly said?" she asked. We said that we could. She hesitated.

"I didn't understand a word," she confessed. "I wonder if what I thought was the Irish language really was just the West Cork accent." We all laughed and Mary and I assured her that this was the case.

"It takes a little time to get used to it," Mary said.

Accent aside, many phrases are translated directly into English from Irish. This gives the West Cork idiom freshness and color—but may be confusing to strangers. For instance, a direct yes or a direct no seldom is used, for they do not exist, I am told, in Irish. Instead, one says "yerra it is," or even, "God it is." For a negative, variations of the same form are used. To say "God it is," is not considered taking the name of God in vain.

"The rural Irish," Father Walsh once told us, "feel the presence of God all the time, so it is natural that they should speak of Him frequently." He said this with a twinkle in his eye. Father Walsh was too wise a man to attempt to change the speech habits of his parishioners.

I asked him if the word Jesus—commonly pronounced Jaysus—also was used in common conversation.

"I remember the Durrus man," said Father Walsh, "who was taking some quite proper English ladies on a tour of the parish. One of them asked if there were many ancient forts in the area.

"'Bless me, ma'am,' he replied, 'the place is aiten with 'em.'" Like a dog with fleas.

An Irish language tense which ordinary English does not contain is used by inserting the word "after." It indicates something quite permanent. When a man is said to be "after dying" it somehow carries the thought that he is pretty dead. Sometimes, however, this form is used loosely. "I am after having a headache" may mean only that the pain is severe, though it may pass.

There is indeed a language barrier. It is not insurmountable but needs climbing. Americans or Englishmen who live in isolated ghettos remain in only limited communication with their Irish neighbors.

Irish attitudes and habits, the products of Irish history, can be very different from those an American would expect. There are class differences both in the United States and in Ireland but the lines of cleavage are not the same.

The area immediately around Dooneen had little direct knowledge of the old Ascendancy. If the habit of pulling a forelock to one's supposed betters ever existed—which I somehow doubt—it has long gone out of fashion. There are, however, some social remnants of the fact that Ireland for centuries was under foreign rule, that the Ascendancy was an upper class with nearly absolute power and that ordinary Irishmen were considered by the Ascendancy to be members of an inferior race. One remnant of this condition, happily receded into history, is an Irish tendency to say whatever a stranger—who may be roughly equated to the old Ascendancy—would want to hear.

A shopkeeper in a rural Irish town may promise goods that he knows cannot be delivered, because he knows you would like to hear him say that you can get what you want. A farmer may make an appointment he knows he cannot keep, and simply fail to show up.

Whether connected with colonial history or simply the product of rural life I am not sure, but time is a different concept in rural Ireland than it is in New York City. It is relatively simple to learn that "evening" means any time after the midday meal. It is more difficult to become accustomed to the idea that "soon" may mean after the passage of a few minutes, a few hours, days, weeks or even months. Events which are promised to take place "soon" may indeed take place, but after you have given up all hope and forgotten about them.

This may be the arrival of goods from a shop, goods no

longer wanted. They may be undesirable for another reason which I suspect is connected with Ireland's colonial past: many jobbers in England, and elsewhere, view Ireland as a dumping ground for inferior goods which they would not attempt to sell in places like London.

Irish farmers, of course, come in a variety of personalities, as do other people. Many, however, are terribly shy. Americans, whose culture seems to encourage them to ask direct questions in loud voices, may meet only embarrassed silence.

When, occasionally, we hired farm boys to help us with the chores, we quickly learned something else: West Cork farming is still a social occupation. The American pattern of a farmer seated on a tractor, alone in a vast field, is not duplicated in Muintirvara Parish. Fields are small. Farming usually consists of a series of small tasks performed by two or more persons working together.

It is unusual to find a West Cork farmer, young or old, who really enjoys working alone. Two men usually will get more than twice as much done as one man.

When a young man was helping us, Mary and I tried to work with him whenever possible. At first I feared this would put us in a master-worker relationship but this was not so. Irish farmers and their sons accept equality with grace and goodwill. On this level the old colonial patterns have been discarded utterly. Because farm work is a social occupation it calls for a tea break in the morning as well as a midday dinner. We learned to enjoy these occasions at least as much as did the young man working with us.

English—or American—residents in rural Ireland who hope to live in baronial style, directing cheap labor from the saddle, as it were, become frustrated and unhappy. There is a considerable turnover of foreign residents with this sort of expectation.

Some Americans, particularly those who cling to their familiar middle-class attitudes and habits, may simply find Irish farmers incompatible. I have my own prejudices here and they are on the side of the Irish farmers. Nevertheless I recognize that real differences may exist, which are not necessarily to the discredit of bourgeois Americans.

One of Mary's old friends from America once went with us to McCarthy's pub on an evening. Later, this friend remarked that "I can't see how you, Mary, with your expensive education, can want to spend your time in such conversation" as that which she had heard in the pub.

There was, it is true, very little in the pub talk that concerned latest trends in art, the ballet, the Broadway theater, etc. One or two men, enjoying leisure time spent with friends, had broken into song.

Most of the time, though, was spent talking on a level that can only be classified as gossip. Such talk concerned the everyday goings-on of people in the parish known to everyone. Events discussed ranged from birth to death, with little left out in between. Farmers also talked about their crops, the prevalence of foxes and the price of pigs.

It was all very concrete stuff without a shadow of pretense. The terms of reference were familiar to everyone. In style, the talk tended to have an ironic edge. This, in addition to the colorful West Cork idiom, gave it a real literary quality, sometimes with poetic overtones.

No matter how much stout was consumed, the absence of profanity and obscenity was notable. A member of the Watch and Ward Society of Boston would not have been offended.

Still, listening to this pub talk one could not help being aware that these farmers and their wives did not have much formal education. No great facility in handling abstract ideas was evidenced. Muintirvara Parish was not ancient Athens.

Schools generally were starved of funds. In Kilcrohane children got chilblains from sitting in a room heated only by a fireplace that served chiefly to warm the teacher. Many farmers said the quality of instruction had fallen over the years. We wondered why they did not insist more vigorously that something be done to improve the schools. This seemed to be another legacy of imperialism. Schools were run by the government and the priests; the old habit of not criticizing these officials persisted.

Meanwhile, priests and government functionaries who knew how bad the schools were seemed powerless to improve them. Responsibility was too divided between the religious and secular authorities.

Under British colonialism an attempt had been made to impose English culture on Ireland. This had been a disaster, for much of the old Irish culture was destroyed in the process, leaving a vacuum. After independence, the attempt was made to fill that vacuum by reviving the Irish language and the culture it once carried. With regret, most intelligent Irishmen came to admit that this was a failure. Use of the Irish language in common intercourse languished; small areas of Irish-speaking populations continued to shrink.

Officially, use of the Irish language was still being promoted with supposed vigor. Most Irishmen and women who had been forced to learn the language in school came to feel it was time wasted. In some schools the attempt to revive Irish included using that language for all instruction. In such schools most pupils failed to learn Irish with any fluency—and consequently failed to learn any other subjects very thoroughly either.

Ireland, I came to believe, was in a period of cultural transition. Out of it, I believed, would come a new cultural fabric, including strands of old Irish, English, American and other influences. These, in the end, would be woven into something with real life and vigor. I thought we were seeing this process at work, on the street, in the pubs and beside the country fireplaces.

Meanwhile, rural Ireland was no place to go for theater, music or the graphic arts. These things did exist. There were even colonies of artists and writers. They were not, however, an indigenous part of the rural Irish scene.

Rural Ireland, finally, could be a profoundly lonely place for some Americans-in-residence. It is not an extension of suburban New York, Detroit or Los Angeles. Muintirvara Parish has one of the lowest population densities in Europe. In all this space one is thrown back upon inner resources; if these are few there is a void. Irish farmers are a friendly and sociable lot but some Americans may have neither the desire nor the capacity for crossing the cultural barriers.

No one can deny the magnificent natural beauty of our parish but I could imagine that even this might add to the feeling of loneliness for some people. Mountains and oceans can be awesome things.

In the new environment Mary and I had chosen for ourselves people tended to be judged by a different scale than that employed in the busy cities of the world. Over and over again we were impressed by the way in which our neighbors, on meeting visitors to Dooneen, ignored titles, academic degrees and social rank. If a man were thought to be friendly and straight he was accepted. Pretense and dishonesty invariably induced our neighbors to retreat behind the barriers.

We tried to make it clear to Americans who approached us with their own projects for building a new life in rural Ireland that in the end they must judge themselves. Only they could know if it would work.

An Organic Whole

❧ "No matter what happens," Mary said one day, "I can never leave Dooneen."

It was a feeling I shared. Neither of us had felt quite the same way about any other place or style of living, certainly not about New York or our careers as journalists.

I had been a dedicated journalist and I remain convinced that it can be an occupation of considerable importance. It was interesting to watch from some favorable vantage points the passing show of current history. I had changed jobs only a very few times in forty years. The possibility of change, on the other hand, was always there. I had advised young reporters to be prepared to quit their jobs at any time. This was, I thought, the only way to maintain journalistic integrity. I still believe this.

Such an attitude, in Dooneen, no longer was possible. When you plant a garden or acquire an animal these things are your permanent responsibility, to the extent that permanence has any biological meaning. You have made a commitment. You may discharge this responsibility well or badly, but to nurture a plant or care for an animal is your problem from then on.

This feeling of commitment was one of the principal ingredients of our new life in Dooneen. Another was the biological reality of imperfection. To be able to accept this and make the best of it was something that I, at least, learned with difficulty. It was an important lesson.

The third ingredient of the new life-structure that was taking shape was the concept of the interrelated wholeness of everything around us and ourselves as a part of it.

This idea no doubt is inherent in all of the major religions of the world. I can only say that for me it developed not out of any abstractions of theology but from concrete, day-to-day experience. In no conventional sense could my feeling about the wholeness of life be called religious. I had merely learned to see a little clearer and to understand a little better the meanings of diverse reality.

The simplest illustration of this is the entirely familiar cycle of feeding animals from the garden and fertilizing the garden with animal droppings. Mary and I were a part of this cycle. The concrete experience of it changed the way we saw ourselves. It also changed the way we looked at animal droppings, which we handled every day and which sometimes found their way into the house.

The more we worked with plants and animals—and the better we came to know ourselves—the more apparent it was that the whole idea of perfection has little meaning in a biological frame of reference. We are not born perfect and we become less so as we grow older. It is the same with plants and animals.

Both the diversity and the imperfection of nature are things to accept, and to work with. To demand perfection can be a destructive thing. The excessive use of chemicals, for instance, in an effort to destroy all insect pests and all weeds can upset a natural balance. In the end, crops, animals and people often are worse off.

Insects develop a resistance to the chemicals. Natural predators of the insects are killed. Weed killers may remain in the soil, altering the structure, killing beneficial bacteria.

No moral absolutes are involved here, however. The careful, limited use of chemicals we found to be sometimes necessary. We always paused to consider the problem as a whole before using any drastic measures against any pest.

We used a spray against potato blight which had been proven in experience by our neighbors to have no harmful side effects. Irish experience with this fungus had been tragic enough. We wished to make no contribution to another Great Famine.

For the most part we used substances of vegetable origin, hence biodegradable. We used nothing that would harm birds; on the contrary, we fed the birds the year around to encourage a large bird population to help us reduce insect damage. We accepted some insect damage and some damage by the birds. A few berry crops we protected from the birds with nylon or wire netting.

As for fertilizers, the goats, rabbits and ducks gave us most of what the garden needed. We added seaweed for potash, ground rock phosphate from North Africa and, selectively, lime. Our soil was full of organic matter. Mulches of spoiled hay, straw and even newspapers added to it.

We did not find it necessary to use chemical weed killers. The Merry Tiller, Dutch hoe, spade and our own hands, plus a fair amount of physical work, took care of the weed problem.

Arch Hill, a remarkable man living near Durrus, taught me something important about weed control: "Always weed your garden before it needs it."

The human dimension of the biological network of which we were a part was, of course, the most important and interesting dimension of all. We had got to know Arch Hill and his wife by accident. Later, they were recommended to us by Father Walsh as "the best sort of Protestants in Ireland."

Arch was an Oxford graduate, an officer both in World War I and World War II—in the British Army—and had been a

schoolmaster in England and a farmer in Wales before coming
to Ireland. He was not young, but kept a fine garden and was
an amusing companion, as was his wife, Bill. The Hills were
without pretense. Their Irish neighbors liked them as much
as we did.

We learned a lot about farming simply by talking to such
people as Arch Hill and Jeremiah Daly. No matter in what
direction our conversations ranged they always came back to
some particular farm problem.

Such a problem was Fleur's horn. Pregnancy had somehow
induced our senior milch goat's horn to renewed growth. It
was in danger of pressing in on her own skull, having turned
at an odd angle. We watched it carefully, day after day.
Finally, Mary and I decided, with Jeremiah's agreement, that
something must be done. We called in Mr. O'Sullivan, a
veterinary surgeon.

Aside from having a good deal of experience with animals
Mr. O'Sullivan was what is known in rural Ireland as a
"whisperer." He has the gift of communicating with animals.
What the scientific explanation for this is I don't know; perhaps there is none. It is, however, an observable fact.

One had only to see Mr. O'Sullivan approaching Fleur, an
excitable animal at best, to know that his relationship with
animals was not an ordinary one. We walked into the goat
house and Fleur eyed us all critically, somehow aware, I have
no doubt, that something unpleasant was afoot. Mr. O'Sullivan
simply spoke to her. She turned to look at him and her expression changed. From then on we had no trouble, though
the operation of cutting off a horn is severe enough.

The worst part, surprisingly, was injecting the local anesthetic. Although Jerry Daly and I held Fleur for the actual cutting part, it was not really necessary. Fleur trusted Mr. O'Sullivan.

The skull itself has to be cut into. There is considerable bleeding. Mr. O'Sullivan treated the wound with antibiotic powder. For several weeks Mary and I kept it covered with an antiseptic salve, which also served to keep flies off. Fleur's milk yield was down for a week or two, but came back again.

We were happy to get rid of the horn, although in one respect it was not entirely successful. It did not come back, as sometimes happens, but on the other hand it did not improve Fleur's temperament. She was still a bully, only so long as she had a sore head she refrained from actually striking Katrina with it. A gesture was enough.

Jerry Daly and Mr. O'Sullivan had thought removing the horn would establish something closer to equality between Fleur and Katrina. They were mistaken. Apparently cows that have been dehorned often are humbled in the process, but goats are different. Fleur remained the undisputed herd leader, even after the herd grew considerably in size.

With animals, as with human beings, behavior problems appeared to be more persistent and more difficult to handle than physical problems. Nor is the behavior of plant life always subject to human expectations, we were learning.

After harvesting our winter garden in the orchard I had removed the remaining black plastic covering and prepared the ground for seeding. We wanted a light covering of orchard grass.

Beneath the plastic sheeting we found that the weeds and all vegetation seemed quite dead, from having been deprived of sunlight. The earth was fine black loam. I rotovated this several times, then raked.

I scattered timothy and white clover seeds over the orchard and harrowed it in and rolled it, using equipment I had constructed for this purpose. The harrow consisted of a heavy plank into which very large nails had been partly driven. The roller was made from a portion of a peeled tree trunk which had floated ashore at Dooneen. These implements were crude, but they worked.

The weather was warm, with frequent light rains—ideal for growing a new lawn. We waited expectantly.

To our dismay what came up was not timothy and white clover but a dense growth of wild mustard.

At first I was inclined to blame the seedsman. What sort of seeds had he sold us? Looking carefully, though, we discovered that timothy and clover had indeed been sown, the seeds had germinated, and young plants were struggling through the earth, beneath the mustard.

When the mustard was in flower the bees were happy, but I was not. We puzzled over this problem for some time before coming to realize what had happened.

The black plastic sheeting, we concluded, had killed the normal competitors of mustard. Mustard seeds are more durable than most. When we removed the plastic sheeting the mustard seed was ready and waiting; it must have sprouted immediately, even before the timothy and clover. Unhampered by its normal competitors, other weeds, the mustard flourished.

I scythed the mustard while it was still in bloom, before new seeds developed. This foliage we used to mulch the Jerusalem artichokes. By keeping the orchard well cut, timothy and clover developed in time. We were able to use this orchard covering to make hay for the goats.

Nature also produced some little unexpected pleasures, that first spring in Dooneen. On a bright moonlight night Mary and I heard a strange sound coming from the field of daffodils grown by Jeremiah Daly as a commercial crop, just above our garden. When I went up to investigate I discovered a frog singing there among the flowers.

I called Mary. We stood in the moonlight, listening to the strange concert, with the daffodils waving in the soft spring breeze.

Frogs are a comparative rarity in Ireland. There are no native toads. How the singing frog got into the field of daffodils we never knew.

There was a sad sequel. One day I saw the ducks tossing a dead frog from one duck to the other. I had seen them kill a mouse in the same way, nibbling it to death as a kind of group sport. It was a cruel end for frog and mouse.

Nature, as has been observed, sometimes is red of tooth and claw. It is not always so. Students of animal behavior have learned that most fierce contests between members of the same species are symbolic rather than bloody.

This, apparently, always has been so, or at least for a very long time. For years naturalists have been wondering why the ancient Irish elk, long extinct, had such large antlers. Specimens twelve feet across sometimes are found in bogs. These antlers cannot have been very useful in combat.

It was concluded that the large antlers on male Irish elks served to impress the females. It took a vigorous male to grow such appendages. By selecting the male with the largest antlers the females were assured of a mate who would impart vigor to the species.

Peat bogs tell a great deal about ancient Ireland. I keep a fragment of oak found in a bog to remind me that the hills we see, now barren rocks and furze and heather, once were covered with spreading oak trees.

Tim Daly, Jeremiah's brother who lived in the townland just west of Dooneen, Cahir, helped me get the fragment of oak from the bog. Our first winter in Dooneen I had bought turf—peat—for burning in our fireplaces from Tim. Owning farmland in Cahir—which means stone fort—gives a farmer the right to cut turf from a bog on the other side of the mountain.

When spring came Tim, who did not own an automobile, suggested that we might help get the turf for the new year by hauling himself and his son, Timmy, from Cahir to the bog, three miles over the mountain on the Bantry Bay side, or perhaps six miles by road. Mary and I took turns at this chore. The bog road traversed barren land. There were no houses; sheep wandered there, and a few wild goats. Below, the wide expanse of Bantry Bay sparkled in the sun.

When he was younger, Tim formerly made the trip over the mountain on foot. When the turf was cut and dried he returned with a donkey, to carry it home in baskets hung from either side of the donkey's back.

A turf bog is a wet place where various vegetation grows, then sinks under water in winter. The water prevents total decay. The result is an accumulated mass of compressed vegetation in which the fiber content is much reduced but the carbon remains. When properly dried it burns slowly, with a fine odor, imparting to the houses and even the clothing and hair of Irish farmers an unmistakable perfume.

For cutting shallow turf, close to the surface, Tim and young Timmy used a hay knife. Deep bogs produce better turf, which, when scooped up with a slane—a particular kind of spade—is little more than black mud. It is heavy stuff to handle. It is spread out in the sun and later stacked, two sods, one leaning against another. Later still it is restacked in larger piles.

Finally it is hauled to Tim's turf shed in a truck owned by Jeremiah's brother-in-law, Paddy Spillane. This is faster and easier than making many trips with a donkey across the mountain. A ride in our van also was easier for Tim and Timmy than walking over the mountain.

"Going to the bog isn't so bad," Tim said, "but walking home again, after cutting turf all day, is tiresome."

For the equivalent of about five-dollars' haulage charge Tim got fuel to heat his house for a year and to do most of the cooking as well.

Turf forms all of the time. There is enough turf on the peninsula to furnish fuel for all of the houses for as long a period as one can see ahead. As the population increases one might think that the turf bogs would be cut out, as some have been in the past. In fact, though, with the advent of oil-fired central heating, cutting turf is declining. Probably turf is being formed faster than it is being cut.

Turf bogs are accorded respect in Ireland, as areas associated with the past. They have furnished fuel for the families in our parish for more hundreds of years than memory and oral tradition can know.

Irish farmers sometimes are criticized for having an excessive preoccupation with the past. We found it, rather, a decent and an appropriate thing.

One evening in Jeremiah's kitchen a discussion arose concerning the little fort of Dooneen, the ancient earthworks just east of the Daly house. An Englishwoman happened to be present. She suggested that she would like to dig in the old fort, hoping to discover there some ancient artifacts, some perhaps made of gold and of great value.

Suddenly the pleasant atmosphere of the Daly kitchen vanished. A dark scowl, such as seldom is seen on Jeremiah's face and is all the more impressive for that, burned from the corner where he was sitting.

"There will be no digging in that fort," he said. It was a verdict from which there could be no appeal. I heartily concurred.

No doubt the Englishwoman put it down to Irish superstition. It is said that if these three-thousand-year-old homesteads are disturbed the fairies will be angry. To me, and I believe to Jeremiah as well, this had nothing to do with it.

One of Jeremiah's pleasures was to sit in a particular spot in the old fort and look out over the bay and to the ocean beyond, while smoking his pipe. One can sit there and imagine how the world appeared to the people who lived there a thousand years before Christ, and who farmed the same land that Jeremiah and I now are farming. There is, I think, such a thing as respect for the past and for the people who lived before us, that is not superstition.

What has happened in the past is a part of the living stream of life that still continues. The interrelated wholeness of life in Dooneen included everything—past, present and future.

Animals Are for Friendship

⊰ Late spring turned to early summer with an Irish ambiguity of warm mists and sunlight. Everything grew—weeds and roses, beans, peas, radishes and also our female goat kid, Joy, who continued nursing not only her proper mother, Katrina, but her adopted aunt, Fleur, as well. Jeremiah continued to disapprove of that and so did I. Mary smiled wisely; it will be all right, she said. I suspected her of applying Freudian ideas to goats, but nothing to do.

As the earth warmed, the green foliage took on a lushness that was almost tropical. Flowers of many colors met the eye everywhere. Mary and I were absorbed by spring, merging with the generality of all of the forms of life around us. It took an effort to remember who and what we had been, before coming to Ireland. The notion that we were an aging couple living in retirement seemed an absurdity. We were, rather, experiencing a new awareness of life, an unfolding, almost a new birth.

In New York we had been encased in steel and concrete and glass. We had moved in a brittle environment of striving and pretense; wealth, power, prestige and position were finely measured. As journalists we could not escape reporting events in terms of the common value system.

We had escaped that trap. We were a part of a different kind of life, biological life, real life, it seemed. We could feel a new sense of freedom in everything we did. Our relationships with all living things were changed. The change was especially notable in the way we related to our domestic animals, the creatures for whom we were directly responsible.

I remember walking one evening with Job, to the top of a hill. There I watched the changes of light as the sun slowly moved behind the horizon, its slanted rays clothing a green field with a luminosity before the field became engulfed in shadows. Then it was the sparkling water of the bay that caught the sun, and finally the mountains across the bay.

Suddenly I realized that Job, beside me, was sharing this experience. No longer was he merely a destructive puppy, a nuisance to be endured. He was a good friend.

One could not pretend that Job would win any prizes for obedience. For that matter, despite his impressive pedigree, he was no show dog; dog breeders do not give away the pick of the litter. Job, though, had become a part of our family and of the total life complex at Dooneen. That fact contributed not a little to my own contentment. I had not enjoyed shouting at Job.

A part of Job's nervousness, we came to understand, was the result of his attempt to follow all of the thoughts and actions of the human community of which he was a part, and to participate fully in it. Intelligent as he was, for a dog, this was asking too much of himself. In the process, however, he developed the ability to sense our moods with great subtlety. In his own way he was more sensitive and understanding than any human being.

Often, as I talked to Job as he followed me when I did the chores, I forgot that he could not talk himself, and looked around, expecting him to answer me. His only comments were barks, whines and growls, and nips with his teeth.

As he came to understand that the use of his teeth, catching hold of our clothing for emphasis, was not welcome, he developed a substitute. He would reach down and pick up a pebble, biting that. He even came to keep a pebble on his favorite Persian rug, in the house, for use in indoor emergencies, when feeling too ecstatic.

Mary and I, in turn, tried to restrain our own habits of laughing too uproariously. Job did not have much of a sense of humor. Loud laughter was something he could not understand and which he found vaguely disturbing.

He liked music, especially string quartets played on our phonograph. Prince, on the contrary, would leave the house whenever we turned on the phonograph.

Job shared the general canine conservatism, fearing all sudden changes or people who were different from the ones he usually saw. One day we had as a visitor a West Indian woman, very black. Job was nearly frightened out of his wits, at first. Then he noticed that she had a pleasant speaking voice and was somewhat calmed.

Finally the woman sang; she was, in fact, a professional singer. Job fell in love. He kept begging for more and more songs. He put his head in her lap as if he were begging for food. When we took the woman to the house where she was spending her vacation, near Kilcrohane, Job insisted on coming with us in the van—and sitting in the singer's lap all the way.

Although friendship was Job's chief function he was a working member of our community as well. He learned to help herd the ducks in at night and was especially useful in finding a duck which had decided, foolishly, to spend the night out. Job would search until he found the wayward duck and then stand pointing until we came.

He barked at all visitors. We learned to identify some visitors by the way Job barked. He chased rats and jackdaws, because he knew we were not overly fond of them.

Sometimes he made me self-conscious by his imitations of me. If I weeded the garden, Job nipped the weeds. If I dug, he dug. When I tied the laces of my boots, Job would sit beside me, grooming his own feet. Sometimes, when I would go around with a pipe in my mouth, Job would pick up a suitable pipelike stick and walk around with it held in his teeth just as I did with my pipe.

Job's relations with Padraic, the tomcat, and with Prince, the Dalys' cattle dog, were complex. Padraic, though he developed into a fearsome hunter, would never bare his claws to Job, although I often wished he would. Job bullied Padraic. Mary said it was a game enjoyed by cat and dog alike. True, Padraic was never harmed.

Prince, however, did not relent in his efforts to try to keep Job from chasing Padraic. As Job grew up, and came to take a more proprietary view of our place, he resented Prince's interference with his sport. Some real fights developed, between the good friends, Prince and Job. I separated them as soon as I could and neither was marked. Padraic seemed to enjoy watching two dogs fight over him.

Aside from catching rats and mice, Padraic was notable for his ability to appear unexpectedly. Mary and I would be walking on the mountain and there the little tomcat would be, beneath a furze bush, meowing his greeting. If I were feeding the ducks, Padraic mysteriously would call to me from a tree beside the duck house. One never saw him coming. Padraic suddenly was there.

When the goats were being milked you could be sure that Padraic would turn up to claim his tithe. In bad weather he often slept in a chair by the fire. If the weather was fine he preferred a hay loft—ours or Jeremiah's.

The ducks were only marginally a part of the human community. Their own community life was pretty intensive. They were willing to suggest being fed—often ahead of schedule— by gathering around Mary or me and making their quiet calls. They helped us by eating quantities of slugs but this, I fear, was for their own benefit rather than ours. When slug hunting took them into the garden they also nipped the lettuces.

The garden was fenced, but the Muscovys were expert fliers. After watching us chase them out, Job got the idea that this was legitimate. He cured the ducks of raiding the garden.

When a duck, chased out of the garden, rejoined the flock in the orchard there was a great ceremony of flock reintegration. The ducks would stand in a circle, facing each other, move their necks back and forth and chatter softly. Perhaps the wayward duck was reporting on her experience; what the other ducks had to say, I couldn't imagine.

The language of the goats was easier to understand. They grunted and called in a variety of tones. The volume of their cries changed with the situation. Mary and I quickly learned to distinguish between sounds indicating alarm, delight, anger, hunger—or just friendliness.

Although we were accepted as honorary members of the herd we felt ourselves under constant scrutiny. The goats seemed to be engaged in a study of the human species and I have no doubt that they understood us better than we did them. They certainly understood by our voices whether we were calling them to come and get food or water, for instance, or were admonishing them for eating forbidden foliage. Each goat knew its name.

As Mary or I approached the pasture one of the goats would see us from some distance; the eyesight of goats is much better than that of most animals. The goat seeing us would first give a grunt to indicate to the rest of the herd what sort of creature was approaching; I have been with the herd as Mary appeared and have witnessed this. The other goats looked up to see for themselves. As our identities became established one of the goats, usually Fleur, called out to us. One cannot say it was a beautiful sound but I never ceased to find pleasure in being hailed by a friendly goat from a distance of a couple of hundred yards.

There could be no doubt that the goats enjoyed our company. In the beginning perhaps it was just that we were associated with feeding and protection. As the human-goat association continued, though, the goats would come to us merely to have their cheeks stroked. They, in turn, would give us little harmless gestures of butting.

This is a goat's way of greeting a friend. Physical contact

seems to be important to most animals. Butting of course also is a means of defense, though this is a different sort of gesture. We got to know the difference—and so did Job. Having been tossed by the goats he later made friends with them and would press his head against one of the goats' head in something approaching mutual affection.

One of the problems in trying to use dogs to manage goats is that dogs tend to become honorary members of the herd and follow the commands of the head goat. Job did learn to help us somewhat in keeping the goats moving along the road, mostly by leading them. If dogs try to move goats by barking at their heels—as dogs move cows—the goats will simply turn around and face the dogs as objects of combat. When we first got goats Prince, from his experience with cows, tried to help us, but quickly gave it up and learned to retire gracefully from the scene whenever we moved the goats.

As summer approached the daylight stretched far into the evening. We often left the goats in the pasture until after 9 P.M., and even after milking would be able to work in the garden for a bit. It seemed a shame to come indoors.

One evening, just as Mary was finishing milking, we heard an automobile drive up outside the gate. I went to see who our visitor was and found Father Keating there in his Volkswagen bug, with a butter box of bees on the seat beside him.

"They are good Irish black bees and behaved well," he said, having traveled with them the thirty miles from Ballydehob.

We were happy to see Father Keating again. We missed his cheerful and understanding presence in the parish after he had been transferred to the next peninsula. We also were happy to see the bees, having almost given up on them. It had been at least six months since we had talked to Father Keating about bees.

"Ballydehob isn't as good as Kilcrohane for bees," Father Keating explained. His hives had been damaged by disease. The bees he brought us were a captured swarm.

Father Keating, Mary and I walked over our land to select a good spot to begin our experiment in beekeeping. We settled on a little plot we called the cherry orchard—three cherry trees were there, surrounded by a rose hedge. It was a spot which was out of the way of ordinary tramping to and fro and the hives could be given a good south exposure. We had only the butter box of bees as a start, but planned on four proper hives eventually.

We found a suitable wooden box to serve as a platform for our new colony of bees, placed the butter box on it, and retired to the house. Father Keating said he would return later, perhaps in a month, to help us tranfer the bees into a proper hive when we had one constructed. We also wanted to wait for a good spell of sunny and warm weather, so that the bees could begin again in their new home, storing honey for the winter.

Over a cup of tea Father Keating told us something of life in his new parish. He had many questions to ask concerning events in our own parish after his transfer to Ballydehob.

How was Michael's experiment with silage going? Was young Jere still courting Lizzie? The conversation moved on to wider issues, world affairs, church affairs—then back to the bees again.

For Mary and me it was the beginning of a long association

with bees, creatures which have fascinated and puzzled many generations of human beings. Bees have a species of intelligence quite unlike that of any other living thing. They dance to tell each other where the best flowers are. They give off a variety of odors each of which apparently communicates vital information.

Individual bees are clever enough. Back of our house we had planted a hedge of broom. Broom flowers resemble sweet peas. At an early stage in the development of these flowers the anthers, containing the pollen, are enclosed in a traplike device. We watched the bees spring the trap by pressing the flower at a certain place. The flowers then opened, the anthers sprang up and the bees gathered the pollen.

A single bee, however, is not a complete biological creature. It cannot live alone. Its life and function relate completely to the colony as a whole.

Key decisions for the colony are, apparently, group decisions. When and where to build new cells, whether to use them to produce workers, drones or queens—or to store honey—are very important questions indeed. How these issues are determined within a colony containing 50,000 honey bees is not easy to understand.

Even to begin to understand bees it is necessary to think of the colony, living in a single hive, as the "organism," and the individual bee as a segment—as the human toe is a segment of the whole human organism. The human toe is a specialized segment of the body; so is the worker, the drone or the queen a specialized segment of the colony of bees. The toe—and the bee—have no real meaning as individual creatures.

An amputated human toe cannot be regenerated. Fortunately, for the bees, a dead queen can be replaced. A cell in which a grub is developing is selected, the grub is given special feeding—and a new queen emerges. The queen, despite her name, is not the leader of the colony. Her specialized function is to be mated—and lay thousands of eggs, each in one cell. It is the life of the colony that is important.

If a human being, or another animal, menaces the colony the bees will sting the intruder without hesitation, although each bee that stings dies as a result of it. The colony lives on.

One may read about bees, but watching them in the garden and in the hive opens a whole new view of life. Getting honey from the bees or eggs from the ducks or milk from the goats became for us merely a useful by-product of an association with the creatures around us. From that association we learned much.

Human beings are not bees any more than they are goats, ducks, rabbits, dogs or cats, but all living things have considerable in common. Interaction between species, within this biological commonality, was an important part of our experience in Dooneen.

We felt about vegetarianism as we did about so-called organic gardening. In general we did not enjoy killing our domestic animals for food, nor did we use chemical pesticides when it could be avoided. Still, we were not cultists. There were occasions when the use of chemicals was indicated. It would be possible to get an adequate protein diet without eating meat or any animal products, but it would be extremely difficult.

Keeping domestic animals certainly interfered with any plans we might have had for traveling. It would have been difficult to find anyone to care for the many animals we had about the place, in our absence. In fact, we had little desire to travel. Mary and I had seen a good bit of the world. Our new life was in Dooneen.

The pleasure of living that life in close association with the animals we cared for seemed to both of us ample compensation for the disadvantages. No way of life is perfect. Ours, we thought, was the best we could devise.

Where Is Dooneen?

❧ Summer in Dooneen was many things. It was the steady hum of bees in the haggard, a sound with special meaning for us because it meant honey in the comb. It was the sight of Michael McCarthy's pretty young daughter, Kathleen, driving the cows down the road and singing as she went. It was an encounter with Jeremiah, as we were taking the goats to their mountainy pasture.

"It'll be a fine soft day on the mountain," he said in his West Cork accent, as if he were chanting the opening lines of an Irish ballad.

The process of acclimatizing ourselves in Dooneen was complex, long, and very nearly a career in itself. We had moved from city to country, from America to Ireland, and to a particular part of Ireland.

During our first winter in Dooneen we had slipped back, for a brief hour, into the world we had left behind us—by visiting a friend aboard the *Queen Elizabeth II* while it was at anchor in Cobh Harbor. To meet the ship we were forced to arise at 4:30 A.M. We drove to Cork City through black darkness. As we boarded the tender which took us out into the harbor a light drizzle was falling out of a dull gray sky.

Aboard the *Queen,* however, lights blazed; plastic, chrome and polished wood glistened everywhere. The passengers seemed to Mary and me, fresh from our rural fastness, to be participants in some fabulous masked ball that had lasted all night. Their faces had an urban pallor seldom seen in Dooneen. Their clothes seemed excessively bright-colored and cut in fashions we had all but forgotten.

We hurried back to Dooneen almost in panic for fear the old life we had glimpsed so briefly somehow would catch us up again. It was the same when we were forced to make trips to Dublin, Cork or Belfast. We outlined our business and duties in advance and went through our paces as rapidly as possible. We always returned to Dooneen gratefully.

Bantry was our nearest urban center, some twenty miles away from Dooneen. It had a population of perhaps 2,000. Shops lined the streets for the equivalent of some six city blocks. From the busiest of these streets you could look up and see cows grazing on the hillside above Bantry.

And yet Mary and I never made a trip to Bantry without experiencing in some degree the same sort of shock of re-entry into urban civilization that we had felt on that visit to the *Queen* or on visits to Dublin, Cork or Belfast. It wasn't only that in Bantry both shopkeepers and shoppers tended to wear shirts and neckties or that in Vickery's pub one could find middle-aged men sipping coffee and tea and studying the stock market quotations in the *Times* of London. There was more politeness in Bantry—and less friendliness.

Kilcrohane had one church, two pubs, one store and the

co-operative creamery, a people-sized town. People who met there knew each other, and each other's families and the condition of each other's livestock and hayfields. In Bantry it was unusual if anyone asked us about our goats. Already, the alienation of an urban place had begun.

Job usually went with us on shopping trips to Bantry. He seemed to enjoy it, but then Job was not forced to walk through the streets and into the shops. He stayed in the van parked along the curbing and watched the passing scene with aloof fascination.

If Bantry was the beginning of city life for us it was the port of entry to the wild back country of the Muintirvara peninsula for most of our visitors or for tourists coming to see the outlandish people and places of West Cork. For these visitors Bantry probably seemed a quaint sort of place, especially on fair days. Then, horses, cattle, sheep and donkeys, and a few goats being sold by tinkers, filled Wolfe Tone Square. Tents were set up in the square where trinkets were offered, and fresh fish. Cattle buyers and sellers met and moved into the nearest pub to conclude the bargain.

If we had to go to Bantry on fair days it merely meant that shopping took longer. We found Bantry in general a depressing place. For one thing, the climate was different although it was only twenty miles distant from Dooneen. When the sun shone in Dooneen, far out on the peninsula, it usually seemed to be raining by the time we got to Bantry. It was colder there.

Bantry is at the head of Bantry Bay, the beginning of inland Ireland. Dominating the town, on the heights above it, is Bantry House, an unhappy reminder of things past. Once the O'Sullivans ruled the whole of this area, Whiddy Island,

Beara Island and the margins of Bantry Bay. They were evicted by the British intruder and the title passed to Bantry House, the seat of the Earls of Bantry, of the English Ascendancy.

With a kind of inverted snobbery, Mary and I never got around to visiting Bantry House, which was open for a fee. The structure, though large and imposing, seemed uninviting. It had no real historic value. It was reported to be in miserable decay. The house is surrounded by some magnificent trees and by a high stone wall of great beauty, enhanced by the collection of ferns, mosses and other growth acquired over the years. The wall and the trees were clearly visible from the road, without paying either of the separate fees charged for an inside view of the grounds and the house.

The shadow of Bantry House fell on the town of Bantry. People there seemed overly impressed by position and place. Certainly there was less of an egalitarian spirit in Bantry than in our own rural parish.

For all its relatively short distance by modern, motorized standards, the leap from Dooneen to Bantry was a long one. In the last generation it had taken farmers the better part of a day to drive their cattle to Bantry for the fair. In the sad years of Irish poverty dispossessed farmers had moved to Bantry desperately seeking food and shelter. The result was a series of shanties and a poorhouse. The contrast with Bantry House was considerable.

There was poverty in our rural parish also in those days, but it was better to live on the land. Those who were able to remain on the land managed to make a meager living somehow, with dignity. Our parish had always been a backwater;

the poor were spared the sight of the rich enjoying their leisure.

For a few brief years after Irish independence Bantry had known relative prosperity, based on fishing and tourism. Then the habits of fish and fishermen changed and Castletown, on the north side of Bantry Bay near the entry, became more of a center for the fishing industry. When the railroad to Cork City was abandoned weekend crowds no longer came to enjoy the scenery and the Bantry strand.

When we first moved to Ireland Bantry, once again, was experiencing a new sort of revival, this time based on the business brought by imported workers building an oil tank farm on Whiddy Island, facing the town in the bay. It was a rowdy and temporary boom. In the end the workers left and the movement of tankers in and out of Bantry Bay tended to discourage tourism.

Oil leaks not infrequently streaked the blue waters of Bantry Bay, killing birds and fish and destroying the nets of fishermen. The American oil company that had built the tank farm sought to placate Bantry by having a statue of St. Brendan erected in Wolfe Tone Square. A disgruntled fisherman told me that if the legend was true, that St. Brendan discovered America, perhaps he was partly to blame for the oil company being there. In any event, the fisherman added, the statue of St. Brendan did not make the oil slicks easier to bear.

In a Bantry bar an old farmer named O'Sullivan told me that he had refused to sell his land on Whiddy Island to the oil company, only to find company trucks ruining the roads and scaring his cattle. He felt very much like the O'Sullivans who had been evicted from the island in the seventeenth century, only this time the Americans had replaced the British as the agents of eviction.

I talked to the American who managed the tank farm. He was impatient of complaining fishermen and regretted the passing of the power of the Ascendancy, as represented by Bantry House.

Incredibly, in the course of our conversation, he remarked that "the Irish have no history." It was, he said, something he had read in *Time* magazine.

The editors of *Time,* I felt, could hardly be held responsible for this opinion. In fact, of course, both Bantry Bay and Bantry House were involved in the eighteenth-century attempt by Wolfe Tone to bring in the French fleet to defeat the British and liberate Ireland. Bad weather scattered the fleet.

A "Protestant wind" blew out of the east, so the jibe went. Like many attempts to reduce history to an aphorism this one ignored the facts—among them that Wolfe Tone himself was a Protestant, and no less of an Irish patriot because of that.

The White family of Bantry House got an earldom out of the incident as a reward for informing the British of the bungled invasion attempt. Remnants of the White family still occupied Bantry House, or parts of it they managed to keep usable, when we first knew Bantry. The roof of Bantry House was said to leak.

Historic events involving Bantry House were strictly peripheral to our peninsular parish. The mainstream was the story of the families on the peninsula—the O'Mahonys, the McCarthys, the O'Donovans, the O'Dalys and the O'Sullivans. The relics of that family history included a series of ruined castles, much older earthworks, caves where priests hid during the persecution and Mass rocks where Masses were said in secret.

The heroism of those long-dead priests is still remembered. So are the tribal disputes among the Irish clans. Both seem more significant in the folk memory than the futile attempts to impose British power and religion. Mass rocks still command respect and reverence. The scenes of the old clan wars are still revisited.

One of these is Carbery Island in Dunmanus Bay, not far from Dooneen. There, in the year 1315, one group of the O'Mahony clan engaged in fierce conflict with another group of the same clan. The folk story describes it as a great slaughter, though Father Walsh, our historian, adds that "Irish annalists, like those of biblical times, wrote in superlatives when it came to a recital of the number killed in battle." Possibly only a few lives were lost.

The O'Mahonys were a proud clan. No fewer than a dozen castles they built in our area still stand in various degrees of ruin. In addition to fighting within the clan there were famous battles with other clans and with the British when they came.

The O'Dalys, traditionally the poets in the courts of the O'Mahonys, held aloof from these struggles for power when they were able to do so. Sometimes, though, they had troubles of their own.

The foundation stones of the home of one of the most famous of the Daly poets, Aohghus O'Daly, can still be seen not far from Dooneen. Aohghus died in 1617 of a stab wound inflicted by an Irish chieftain who resented what he had written. As a former journalist whose writings had not always been appreciated by those whose actions I had described, I was especially drawn to Aohghus O'Daly—the more so because he was related to my friend Jeremiah.

The O'Dalys had a famous bardic school just east of us along the shores of Dunmanus Bay. There, so it was said, one of the sons of the King of Spain studied—and was drowned in the bay while swimming.

Our peninsular history included at least one famous romance, involving a Catholic priest and Protestant girl. He was Father Daniel McCarthy. She was Sarah, daughter of Captain Blair, whose name was given to Blair's Cove near the head of Dunmanus Bay.

Captain Blair, forced to be away from home for long periods, made Father McCarthy the guardian of his daughter. What happened in the course of this association between the priest and his ward has been lost to history—what walks they took along the bay, picking sea pinks and primroses; what birds sang for them; the clouds that billowed above the mountains and the sunlight that sparkled on the water. All we know is that in the end, Daniel McCarthy left the priesthood and he and Sarah were married.

Comments Father Walsh, with ecumenical fairness, "Of this union came a goodly company of distinguished dignitaries in the Anglican Church."

Nothing, of course, is really lost to history. Much of the history of Muintirvara still lives in oral tradition. The relics still stand, among them some magic wells, the water of which is still thought by some to have curative powers. Another is the ogham stone which I found in a hedge and now stands on top of a bookcase in the corner of our living room.

These Irish relics somehow seem more meaningful than

the evidences that the British passed this way. Toward the end of our peninsula is one of the towers the British built when an invasion by Napoleon was feared. The invasion never came. There are no stories to tell about the tower; it simply is there. Dermot Daly's cows graze around it.

The liberation of Ireland from British rule formed the subject matter of ballads and recitations which we heard in McCarthy's pub on a Sunday night when we first came to Dooneen. A handful of West Cork veterans of that fight were still to be met.

Michael Collins, the military leader of the successful liberation of Ireland, has been elevated by time to a place beside Finn macCool, the legendary hero-giant of prehistoric Ireland. In folklore, time telescopes easily.

Resting from the chase, so the older legend goes, Finn macCool lay down on Seefinn Mountain, the highest peak of Muintirvara peninsula. So big he was that he took up the whole of the mountain for his resting-place. His hounds—built on the same scale as their master—lay down on the mountain ridge to the west of Seefinn, Ahileague, just above Dooneen.

Michael Collins was so young, so much the simple West Cork farm boy, that his true stature was not fully recognized until some time after his death. He suffered from his admirers, who tended to talk and to write about him as a romantic, fearless desperado. He was that, perhaps, but he also was a hardheaded realist. Other Irish heroes had led glorious defeats; Collins found the difficult road to victory.

In his Clonakilty office, Michael Collins' nephew, Liam Collins, once showed Mary and me the penciled notebooks kept by his uncle when he was leading the Irish struggle for independence. When these scrawled words were written Michael Collins was forced to move his headquarters from place to place; the British had put a high price on his head. He remained the responsible leader—and also found time, as the notebooks showed, to make meticulous notes on expenditures for such humble items as feed for horses and men and petrol for lorries. In history he emerges as a cautious bookkeeper as well as a swashbuckling soldier; it is not a bad combination.

The assassination of Michael Collins in the civil war that followed the fight for independence was one of those senseless acts that reveal the sordidness of mediocrity in the presence of the superior man. There are similarities in the deaths of Abraham Lincoln and Mahatma Gandhi. Collins was killed because he sought to turn the Irish nation from war to peace.

But in the legends of Muintirvara, Michael Collins still lives. He is a figure no smaller than Finn macCool—and sometimes even seems to merge with Finn macCool as one looks up to Seefinn Mountain when the clouds are gathered there and the wild goats leap from rock to rock.

Finn macCool and Michael Collins both helped define the Ireland we knew. All of Ireland was outlandish, in a literal sense—the western extremity of Europe. Our corner of Ireland was the westernmost outpost of the Irish extremity. The better we came to know it the more we came to realize it was no ordinary place.

There were fewer kinds of plants in Dooneen than in most of Europe. There were more of each of the species that were there. In many ways Dooneen, with its mists and fog and its ocean winds, was more a part of the North Atlantic than of Europe.

Where Is Dooneen?

The great Atlantic seals were our neighbors. The O'Mahonys, having fought their battle on Carbery Island and left, the seals then took over. They often swam around the shores of Dooneen. On a quiet night in late summer you could hear them singing.

Of Milk and Honey

꒰ It seems to be in the nature of man that if you give him milk and honey he asks for champagne and caviar. Mary and I did, in fact, make caviar out of herring roe; our bee balm "wine," when bottled a little prematurely, had a sparkle to it. For a steady diet, though, we found milk and honey best. Milk meant goats; honey meant bees.

After kidding, Fleur gave about a gallon of milk a day and Katrina only slightly less. She was a better goat, by breeding, but it was her first kidding. We drank milk, fed milk to the rabbits, to Job and to Padraic. Mary made cheese. We might have been satisfied but, being human, I was not. I begrudged the milk that Joy took, nursing beyond her time.

Despite Mary's collaboration with this arrangement I was determined both to increase our own supply and to further Joy's development as a converter of green foliage to protein by weaning our attractive young female goat. I went about this project in a fairly organized, not to say plodding manner.

Mary helped, tongue in cheek, obviously getting some amusement out of my efforts.

Some years previously, while visiting Jedda, Saudi Arabia, I had seen milch goats roaming the dusty streets, accompanied by their kids. To keep the kids from sucking, the Arab goat keepers had fitted them with brightly colored cotton cloth brassieres. What worked for the Arabs, I argued, might work as well for a couple of Americans farming in Ireland.

In an American goat journal we had seen an advertisement for goat brassieres. They were an adaptation of a device sold to cowmen for use in weaning calves. At some considerable expense and trouble we obtained two of these, one for Fleur and one for Katrina. They were made of heavy canvas and came equipped with an intricate set of straps for fastening them in place, around the udders.

I can only think that the people who made them had seen a picture of a goat but had had no acquaintance with the real animal. By variously adjusting the straps I tried to make them fit; they didn't. Joy simply nuzzled beneath the brassieres and got her usual quota of milk. The only result of putting the brassieres on the milch goats was that Joy spilled a little milk in getting hers.

Mary, always on the side of the goats, pointed out that not only were the brassieres doing no good but in time they might well chafe the milch goats, causing sores. I took off the brassieres and put them on a shelf in my closet, a place reserved for many useless objects such as a radio beyond repair, a pair of sun goggles and a World War II battle jacket.

The brassieres did provide a subject of conversation in McCarthy's pub, which I was told had its bright moments. Unfortunately, Irish farmers were too polite to make their comments in our presence and we missed the full flavor of it.

I did ask the pub crowd of farmers what they did when a calf continued nursing beyond a reasonable period. They said they used a leather muzzle.

It wasn't clear to me how a muzzle was to be constructed that would allow Joy to browse on furze and heather without also allowing her to nurse. I took the problem to a Bantry harness maker, who suggested a nose strap with spikes. The spikes, he said, would annoy the milch goats, when Joy attempted to nurse, and they would kick her away.

When the harness maker had done his bit the result was formidable. The spikes were long and sharp. Mary was indignant.

"It would be much better to lose our entire milk supply to Joy," she said, "than risk hurting the udders of Fleur and Katrina with that thing." In fact, she repeated, we were getting enough milk as things were.

Unwilling to dismiss still another investment in a weaning device without a trial I clipped off each spike and filed it blunt. Mary still looked at it with suspicion but agreed reluctantly to let me put it on Joy's muzzle and see what happened.

Joy wore the thing as if it were a piece of feminine frippery. Gaily she arched her pretty neck—and sucked away, not touching the udders with truncated spikes.

The spiked muzzle was hung in the milking shed, like a relic of the Inquisition.

Finally I drove to Durrus with an elaborate design for a gate frame to be used in the goat house, penning off Joy from the milch goats at night but keeping her visually in contact with the other goats. It was to be no ordinary gate but made to fit over and around an existing wooden bench.

Paddy O'Donovan, the blacksmith, squinted at the piece of paper, asked a few pertinent questions and agreed to make the strange object. When completed, in iron, it was heavy and an awkward load for our little van. Most of it hung outside the back doors as I drove to Dooneen. There I covered the frame with welded wire mesh, fastened carefully so the goats could not easily paw it off.

Joy didn't seem to mind being penned off at night. Being exclusive appeared to please her; she could take her time eating her carrots and the other goats couldn't steal any. Of course she continued to nurse in the daytime, when the goats were in their pasture. The morning milking got all of the available supply, however, and that portion of the milk going to Mary and me was increased a bit.

Our bookkeeping did not include the cost of the devices, unsuccessful and marginally helpful, which we had tried in order to reduce Joy's nursing. If that cost had been charged against the additional milk we obtained I fear it would have turned out to be fairly expensive stuff.

So we had milk. We also had bees—but as yet no honey.

A few weeks after Father Keating brought us the butter box of black bees, however, he returned to see how they were getting on. Meanwhile, following his instructions, I had constructed some beehives. Each of these consisted of four pieces of wood nailed together to form a sort of box, but open top and bottom. The inside dimensions were 15 inches by 17 inches by 8½ inches deep. There was a separate bottom board on which the open-ended box rested and a removable top board and a waterproof cover over that.

For the inside of the boxes I put together frames in which wax sheets had been inserted—a dozen frames for each box. In time I constructed eight complete boxes, each equipped with wax-sheet frames. These were to house four colonies of bees, each colony having an upper and a lower apartment, inter-connecting.

The idea of such elaborate housing is that the bees will build their combs on the wax sheets. Each frame can be removed. The whole colony can be inspected from time to time in detail. Honey can be taken a little at a time, and only if there is seen to be enough for the bees themselves.

If the bees make too many queen cells, in preparation for swarming, excess queen cells can be removed. This discourages swarming; excessive swarming reduces the population of workers and the production of honey.

Dooneen and the surrounding area is ideal honey country, with a mild climate and many flowers, some of which bloom the year around. Many farmers in the area had kept bees at one time or another. They had, however, used straw skeps, the traditional domed beehives. They are nice to look at, but in order to get honey the bees must be driven out of the hives and the entire lot of honey taken, leaving none for the bees. Some-times the bees are all killed in the process of getting honey. Sooner or later farmers using this wasteful method—and ac-cumulating a few bee stings—gave up keeping bees.

Father Keating was trying to convince farmers that they should return to beekeeping, but use more modern equipment and rational methods.

Perhaps Father Keating thought that if Mary and I learned to manage bees successfully the demonstration might induce others to try it, too. Beekeeping by modern methods did catch on to a limited extent. Father Keating's own beekeeping was the best demonstration of all. He was extremely generous in helping other beekeepers.

When he returned to look over our first colony, in the butter box, he discovered that the bees had developed a new brood and had begun to store honey. It was, he said, time to move them to the new quarters. He, Mary and I each put on veils and gloves and stuffed our trousers into rubber boots; bees climb upward and it is unwise to have pants legs hanging open at the bottom. We got a smoker going.

Quieting the bees with smoke, we overturned the butter box gently and placed one of the hive boxes on top of it, over the open end. Fortunately the two boxes fitted well. Then we pounded vigorously on the butter box, which had the effect of driving the bees upward, in this case into the proper hive fitted with wax frames. It took a bit of doing to induce them to leave their old combs but they did.

As he worked with the bees Father Keating talked gently to them. He was, I thought, particularly persuasive when two of the bees got inside his veil and began crawling over his nose.

"Aisy . . . aisy, my friends," he said. "You be good to me and I'll be good to you."

He was very careful not to injure the bees in transferring the swarm. Aside from Father Keating's love for bees, he pointed out that a crushed bee apparently emits an odor that alarms all of the bees in the vicinity, making them more likely to sting.

The last step was to remove the butter box entirely and to

place the hive box on its own floor board. A few of the bees remained in the butter box, but the queen was among those which had ascended into the hive, so that all of the bees finally joined her, with the exception of a few stragglers. Father Keating carefully picked bees out of honey that had been spilled in the overturned butter box; bees can drown in honey.

Taking the butter box indoors, we removed the combs and put them into large glass jars. We all tasted some and agreed it was excellent, compounded of the nectar of many flowers. From the butter box we obtained about fifty pounds of honey.

"You could have been keeping bees for years and not done as well," said Father Keating.

We did remove some brood cells, containing bee grubs, but were not excessively particular about this. A few grubs, we reasoned, would add to the protein content of the honey.

That night Mary made pancakes, which we drenched in honey, with milk to drink as well.

As farmers who had kept bees in years past came to taste our honey they said it had the real "old-time flavor." They attributed this to the fact that it had come from a butter box hive—and not from a modern hive equipped with its own wax frames. We tried to point out that the wax sheets, used in the frames, are simply beeswax, compressed from combs after the honey has been extracted.

"You can't buy honey like this in Bantry," they insisted.

Having achieved milk and honey one might have thought our problems were solved. Life, unfortunately, is not quite like that. Aside from the limitations of our own, human condition, the creatures furnishing us with milk and honey showed a deplorable reluctance to conform to our convenience.

When Mary drove to Shannon Airport to pick up her mother, who was coming for a visit, the difficulties inherent in the life of milk and honey struck me with full force. I was left on my own to cope with the plants and animals and with all of the vagaries of nature as best I could.

It is not true, I discovered, that one person can perform the routine tasks on a farm in only twice the time it takes two. Working together, Mary and I had achieved a fair level of efficiency. When I was left alone I often did these same tasks badly, frequently retracing my steps; the old routine was broken. Job and I trotted from rabbit house to garden to goat pasture and back again in an endless round of feeding, watering, harvesting and weeding.

Mary had done all of the milking in the past. I now discovered that my hands were too big for the teats of the goats —and my patience too small. Still, I had no choice: the goats had to be milked-out twice in the thirty-six hours Mary was away. Otherwise their milk production would be down from then on.

There was some random squirting. My hands and arms got very tired. I perspired. Mary had milked each goat in about five minutes; it took me more than half an hour. I did get all of the milk there was, though, as determined by weighing the output.

Like most men left on their own I cut corners in getting my own lunch. Mary had left some of her own Irish soda bread. I obtained some lettuce from the garden and added peanut butter. This, with a glass of goats' milk, was it.

Which was fine enough until I noticed a fat slug crawling out of my sandwich and across the plate. Apparently my washing of the lettuce had been less than thorough.

While dealing with the slug I heard a sort of roaring noise, coming from behind the house. Investigating, I found a swarm of bees gathering in a strawberry tree. The branch on which they had settled was bending low. Still a novice with bees, I longed to call for help, but no help was available—and besides, at any moment the bees might decide to leave the strawberry tree and depart altogether.

I ran back into the house and put on my veil and gloves. I found an extra hive, prepared with wax sheets in frames. How to get the bees from the strawberry tree into the hive? I tried to remember what I had read in the bee book, and what Father Keating had told me. I placed the hive just under the swarm, on a slight elevation. Then I got a wide board and placed it as a sort of ramp, leading upwards from the ground to the hive entrance.

Then I shook the bees gathered on the branch of the tree and they fell onto the ramp. So far, so good. I squatted beside the bees and watched.

First a few of the bees entered the hive while the rest clustered on the ramp, apparently waiting the verdict. Then the exploring bees came out of the hive and went back in again with a few dozen followers. Still, the main clusters waited outside.

At that point a strange thing happened. Perhaps eight or ten bees formed a chain, head-to-toe, leading from the hive entrance down the ramp. In this position they began a furious beating of wings. Soon the front rank of the waiting swarm began to break away; a moment later the whole swarm was in motion. The chain of bees kept fanning their wings while the swarm passed around them and into the hive.

Later I read that the fanning bees had been wafting an odor to the waiting swarm which was the signal for their movement into the hive. I was inclined to believe this, although the whole question of how bees communicate seems to be in dispute.

Meanwhile, with Jeremiah's help I carried the hive to the cherry orchard and put it on a platform some distance from the first hive. We now had two colonies of bees to gather honey for us.

I returned to my lunch only to be disturbed a second time, by the same, now-familiar roaring of a swarm of bees. This was too much! My first thought was that the swarm I had captured had left their new home, and I ran to the cherry orchard; the swarm had not left and the bees already were gathering nectar and pollen.

When I discovered the new swarm it was high in a hedge. To capture it as I had the first one seemed impossible, so instead I used a plastic pail. Climbing up a stepladder, I placed the pail beneath the swarm and shook the bees into it. Then I covered the pail with a cloth.

Taking the captured bees to the cherry orchard, I used the sloping-ramp technique to induce the new swarm to join the colony previously captured and housed. What mutiny there was I put down with puffs of smoke from a bee smoker. It worked.

In my excessive pride of accomplishment, however, I attempted to feed the integrated colony some sugar syrup without putting on my veil and gloves again—and was rewarded by a severe bee sting on my forehead. When Mary returned she got the stinger out, but the headache was there.

So much for milk and honey.

A Year Is Only a Beginning

> We were surprised when the English family which had been blocked in the lane by the moving van when our household goods arrived, returned to Dooneen to pay a call. It was August again. The time for their annual holiday had come around once more. They stayed for dinner.

Dick and Joy Knowler and their children, now rapidly becoming adults, were pleasant people, intelligent and decent. They liked Ireland and the Irish, but some of their friends back in England, they said, had advised them against returning to Ireland—because of the "troubles up north."

"But there are no such troubles here," I assured them. Perhaps I did not really feel as certain as I tried to sound.

On two or three occasions my old newspaper had asked me to go north to write articles for them on the situation. That conflict was ugly enough.

When Ireland obtained its independence, six counties in the northeast, a part of the province of Ulster, remained under British rule. This enclave was carved out so that the Protestants

[267]

—a minority in the whole of the Irish island—would have a local majority and in the six counties the Catholics would be the minority. This allowed the Protestants, or the leading segment of the Protestants, to remain in the same position of paramount power and prestige that had been enjoyed by the old Ascendancy in the whole of Ireland under British hegemony.

Times, though, had changed. The Catholic minority in the north of Ireland, like the black minority in the United States, no longer was willing to accept a position of permanent inferiority.

This was the basis of the conflict. Mary and I unavoidably were sympathetic with the underdog in this, as in all similar situations in the world. At the same time we could not but regret the rising tide of violence. Repression of the aspirations of the minority was met by attempts to throw off that repression by any means available. As effective peaceful demonstrations were curbed, the available means tended more and more to include guns and bombs. Finally both Protestants and Catholics in the six counties found themselves involved in almost random acts of violence, with the British Army attempting to hold on the lid, with indifferent success.

Every time I had returned from a trip to Belfast I was amazed how small an impact the troubles in the North had made on life in our parish. Muintirvara Parish was, of course, in the extreme south of Ireland—but it was all one island and not a very big one at that. We did hear vague rumors of some harassment of the English elsewhere in County Cork; there were no serious incidents in our parish. Trouble in the North seldom was mentioned.

Relations between the Irish and the English in the parish

were difficult for Mary and me to understand. The cliché, a love-hate relationship, seemed almost to fit. Irish resentment of the English was matched by Irish pleasure at English praise. One Englishwoman in our area was the most fervent supporter of IRA violence in the North. English families moved to West Cork—and returned to England again, after selling out to other English families. There was more eccentricity than consistency in the pattern of Anglo-Irish relations.

Like most of the families in the parish, Mary and I had more to do than to worry much about the troubles in the North, or relations with the English, residents or visitors, in County Cork. On the whole we found the English very much resembling the rest of the human race, which is to say that they were a mixture of good, evil and indifference.

After the Knowlers had visited us on a return engagement, and we realized that we had in fact been living in Dooneen for a whole year, Mary and I tried to take a fresh look at Muintir-vara Parish. Since we had first visited the parish, some three years before, it had indeed changed somewhat. Chiefly, I suppose, there were more automobiles, television sets and bathrooms in the parish. The people were looking outward a little more, especially the young people.

On the other hand, horses still outnumbered tractors. About as much cooking was still done over turf fires as on gas stoves or by electricity. Strangers and summer people had built a few little houses called bungalows, but most houses were still traditional farm dwellings like our own—stones piled up with clay, plastered outside and in, roofed with slate. To say of a man that he had a slate missing was still understood to mean that his brains weren't functioning as they should be.

You could still get a good conversation going in the pub by

talking about the differences between one kind of turf and another or the value of hay cut early or cut late. Sunday morning Mass was a gathering of Kilcrohane that still represented the community as a whole.

During our second August in Dooneen, Jerry Daly asked me if I would help him by hauling his milk to the creamery in our van for a week or so. The Dalys, since they had purchased a car, usually hauled the milk in a trailer hitched behind the car. Temporarily, Noel Daly would be needing the automobile, for his work was taking him a dozen miles away, to another creamery in the same co-operative.

It pleased me to haul the milk to the creamery. The morning gathering of the farmers there was comparable to Sunday Mass as an act of community solidarity. It was good to observe from the inside the pattern of mutual help, as farmers assisted each other with the heavy milk cans, called churns. There were no pleases and thank-yous. It was all within the family; it had always been done this way.

I had observed the same undemonstrative spirit of mutual help in digging potatoes, making hay and threshing oats. As we were included in these tasks we felt more a part of the community.

It would not be truthful to say that there were no differences between ourselves and our neighbors. We were the Yanks, with strange accents and strange ways. We would always be different. After the first year, though, our differences were accepted. When our neighbors talked of strangers and foreigners they tacitly excepted Mary and me.

We had planted, cultivated and harvested crops. Our ducks had hatched a new generation, our rabbits had kindled, our goats had kidded and our bees had swarmed. Somehow Mary and I had coped with these events as our neighbors had learned to cope with burgeoning life on their own farms. This, like the calluses on our hands, helped to establish us as members of the community.

Some farmers cut enough turf so that we could buy some for our own fires. We knew which farmers would be likely to have oats to spare—and where to go to have the oats ground so that we could blend the grain in the feed concentrates for our goats. I took a particular pleasure in taking sacks of oats to the mill in Drimoleague, watching it be ground, and taking the "bruised oats" home again; such a thing had farmers done since ancient times. We developed sources for hay and for straw, when we needed these things; farmers saved a little extra so that we could have some.

Whenever we went anyplace in the van we always picked up someone—and it was someone we knew. If people didn't want a ride they waved anyway as we passed, and we waved back. We learned the necessary art of waving without losing a grip on the steering wheel. We often stopped the van along the road to talk to someone. Vehicles stopping so the drivers could have a chat, or cows meandering, halted what traffic there was along the narrow roads. Other things were more important than getting places on time.

As we learned to accept the changeable weather we also learned to accept the changeable temperaments of some of the people in the parish. Winston Churchill used to talk about British phlegm—imperturbability, which he counted a virtue. It isn't an Irish virtue on all occasions. People quarrel and make up and live to quarrel again. What may seem to be immutable often isn't.

One farmer we knew had courted the same girl for fourteen

years, a not uncommon thing to do in rural Ireland. He never asked her to marry him, assuming she would do when he was ready.

When he did get around to asking her—she refused him. It was a blow from which he never really recovered.

To say that within our first year we learned to accept everything Irish wouldn't be true. We could never quite understand the way many Irish farmers refused to complain, even when complaints were, in our eyes, more than justified and might well have done some good. For instance, we did not approve of the way children were switched or whacked in some schools. Most parents did not approve, either, and this form of punishment did nothing to further education. Parents, though, were extremely reluctant to make any protest. There were other examples. A bad priest or a bad agricultural adviser in any part of rural Ireland could do a great deal of harm—unchecked.

These remnants of colonialism, we assumed, would fade in time. We hoped that the good in rural Ireland would remain at least as long as we did.

There were exceptions among the general inclination by West Cork farmers to accept what those in authority decreed for them. One such exception was a farmer named Tadhg ODonnabhain, living near the village of Kilcrohane. In middle age, and with the most meager educational preparation, he decided that he wanted a college education.

When he presented himself at the university in Cork City he found the professors sympathetic, but the administration greeted his request for admission with discouragement and skepticism. There were, after all, the authorities said, formal requirements for university entrance—requirements he lacked.

He was expected to leave, cap in hand, and go back to his cows and his hayfields. Tadhg, however, not only had taught himself to read Irish and had read a great deal in that language, and in English; he also had studied the fine print in the university's rules and regulations.

If a prospective student was able to pass prescribed examinations, he pointed out to the authorities, formal requirements of scholastic preparation might be waived. No one quite knew how to handle this middle-aged farmer from the backcountry. Perhaps because they didn't know what else to do they gave him extensive oral examinations—and he entered the university. After he obtained his degree he combined farming in our parish with teaching Irish language and history in Bantry.

It was always a pleasure to have Tadhg drop in for tea. Tadhg and I were not, however, always in agreement.

He firmly believed that the old culture of Ireland should be revived. This only could be done, he further believed, if the Irish language were substituted for English in Ireland.

I doubted if this were desirable. I was fairly certain it was impossible.

In honesty, I also had to admit that I was not eager to make the effort of becoming fluent in the Irish language. Our farmer neighbors were no more willing to do this than I was.

English was the means by which Irishmen had come to communicate with each other, except for a tiny minority. The old Irish language had enlivened Irish-English. The Irish idiom had enriched the English language for Americans, British and others. The English language was rich in literature, a flexible, subtle and precise instrument in expert hands.

Tadhg and I came closer to agreement on Irish politics.

He shared the sympathy Mary and I had for the underdog Catholics in the North. Being Irish, and a special sort of Irishman, Tadhg had more nearly orthodox Republican (in the Irish use of the label) views than we could have. This did not mean that he was in favor of blowing things up in Belfast— by no means all Republicans favored this procedure, though the most violent wing of the IRA also called itself Republican. The bombers and the gunmen on both sides were a small fraction of the whole people, even in the North.

On the other hand Tadhg was an exception, in our parish, in his deep interest in events in the North. He believed the government in Dublin was not doing all it might do to help the Catholic minority in the six counties.

The more we talked, however, the more the problem of Northern Ireland seemed to defy human wit to solve. Whatever our disagreements, Tadhg was never in ill humor with Mary and me. As an unusually articulate West Cork farmer he was extremely helpful in our efforts to understand the views and feelings of the people among whom we were living.

When visitors came to Dooneen from Dublin they sometimes talked of the danger that troubles in the North would spread to the rest of Ireland. They even talked of the possibility of a new civil war, engulfing the whole of the island.

It was not a happy thought for Mary and me—and at least on the surface of things seemed totally unreal in our parish. Life jogged on. It was easy enough to ignore the rumble of thunder from the North.

Late in every summer Kilcrohane had its annual carnival, when nearly everyone in the parish gathered for a day or two of fun and games in a field back of the co-operative creamery.

There were footraces, donkey rides, many games, parades and dances. The curate of Kilcrohane set up committees to manage the event.

The high point, this year, was the horse race, which, as it turned out, was something few in the parish would be likely to forget soon. It was an ambitious try; running horses around that small field, while small children dodged about, was not something that appealed to most farmers. Only three entries could be found.

One of them was a blooded stallion belonging to an Englishwoman who took her horses seriously. Her eldest son was to ride it. To give her younger son some experience, she also entered a donkey, with that boy astride.

The only other entry was Fox, a horse with a reddish tint to his coat, with Con Lehane riding. Con was a farmer who had a part-time job working on the roads in Kilcrohane. Fox was a familiar sight in the village as he pulled a cart into which Con shoveled road scrapings.

What had begun as an attempt by a young curate to sponsor a horse race to enliven the carnival thus developed into a good-natured parody of the "troubles up north." Irish farmers are too polite to have shouted political slogans on such an occasion. Still, there it was: the English vs. the Irish all over again.

There was much grinning as the entries were lined up. In view of the obvious inequality of the participants, betting on the outcome was less than lively. One could not say that the interest was the less for that. There was the usual hushed attention just before the shout went up: "They're off!"

There was a good deal of confusion; in the excitement of it all it wasn't easy to see just how everything happened.

Suddenly it became clear that the boy who had been riding the blooded stallion had been thrown. A cry went up: was he hurt? No, he picked himself up and walked off.

His mother, plainly furious, rushed out into the arena, caught the stallion and herself leaped to the saddle, to complete the race. But meanwhile, the donkey, accustomed to following the stallion, had halted beside that horse while it changed riders.

Undistracted, Con Lehane and Fox galloped on. The cart horse and the Irish farmer came in the easy winners.

Con smiled broadly as he collected the prizes—an electric blanket and a five-pound note. Sure and it was a grand, brave day for the Irish altogether.

Shades of Black

❧ "Whatever happens," said the ten-year-old daughter of one of our neighbors during a family discussion of general economic conditions, "Mary and Donald will be all right. They have everything they need, right there in Dooneen."

It was a kind thought and a pity it wasn't true. We did try, by subsistence farming and household processing, to come as close as possible to feeding ourselves. We succeeded, thereby, in living well on a very small income. That we were independent of the world outside Dooneen we never imagined. On several occasions our electricity supply was cut off and the reality of our dependence became more than apparent.

Disasters of various shades of black threatened with a fair frequency. We met them as best we could because we had to. There were times when only Job's patient sympathy, the brave song of the mistle thrush—and Mary's unquenchable optimism—stood between me and despair.

When the ducks stopped laying, as ducks will, we bought a battery-cage to house four hens and put it in one of the outhouses. Since the cages were largely automatic this added little to our chores and the cost of feed was not too high. We had enough eggs once more.

As crises went, this was minor, though eggs were a chief source of protein. Getting the automated cage and hens of assured laying ability was not altogether easy, however; few such things were, we found, when one lived in so sparsely settled an area.

The cage, an ungainly affair, was shipped to Bantry. Mary and I picked it up with the van but discovered it was too big to fit inside. We roped the cage on top of the van. On the way home we stopped for tea with friends along Bantry Bay and in approaching their house one of the legs of the cage became entangled in a hedge, breaking off.

We found the hens advertised in a newspaper. They were sent by bus to Bantry, after considerable negotiation with the bus people. When we picked them up we found four miserable creatures crammed in a cardboard box. The hens, furthermore, were suffering from lice and were all but denuded of feathers.

A little amateur carpentry repaired the cage. Mary's skill as a vet proved adequate to destroy the lice without hurting the hens. They were good layers.

Rabbits became ill of unknown diseases. Veterinary surgeons knew nothing of rabbits—even less than they did about goats. At first we tried to treat sick rabbits ourselves, bringing them into the house. If they were very ill we kept them in the bathroom. They usually died anyway. The bathroom inevitably became a pretty messy and depressing place.

In the end we were forced to accept the advice of most of the literature on raising rabbits and kill them promptly when they became ill, so diseases would not spread. I did not enjoy killing rabbits under any circumstances. Killing a sick rabbit seemed a particularly disagreeable form of euthanasia.

When our bees first swarmed we thought ourselves reasonably clever to have captured and housed them. The next spring we proceeded to let them starve to death. An early period of warm weather, encouraging the bees to begin brood activity, was followed by a cold, damp spell. Brood activity created demands for honey greater than the stored supply; the weather prevented the bees from gathering new nectar. Had we known more about bees, and been sufficiently vigilant, we could have fed them over this period.

Our cabbages developed clubroot, a condition we had not anticipated; the plants withered and some died. We consulted the government agricultural expert, who recommended a complex chemical treatment which we wished to avoid if possible. Then a farm woman in the parish whom we met along the road suggested dipping cabbage plants in hydrated lime as they were planted out. This worked. Cabbage fly—and carrot fly—were something else. We tried planting onions nearby, as suggested by a book on organic gardening. It didn't work. We shifted planting times around but finally came to accept a certain amount of damage.

The farmer who had been supplying us with turf to burn in the fireplaces decided he could do so no longer because his son, who usually dug the turf, went to London. While arranging for a new source of turf we found a farmer who had thinned a grove of holly trees and bought some logs from him. Holly wood makes a fine fire, though in parts of rural England it is believed that it is bad luck to burn this wood.

Ireland is more enlightened. Prejudice against burning holly

wood is known to be a Druidic remnant. On the other hand, yew trees are sacrosanct in Ireland: One man's meat . . .

On more than one occasion when foxes were lurking about, one of our ducks mysteriously disappeared. This was frustrating, as Mary and I were about as fond of foxes as of ducks. We did try to get all of the ducks in well before dusk but a hungry fox is a bold creature—especially a vixen with cubs to feed.

The loss of a duck, however, was nothing compared to the morning we went downstairs, after an unusually wet gale from the east, to find the living room flooded with water. I put on my rain gear and went out into the weather, the gale still raging, to investigate the cause of the flooding under our east wall. There, in the orchard, was a mistle thrush, facing the wind, singing his heart out. From then on stopping the flood coming into the house became possible.

Ultimately, it involved a new concrete drain along the east wall of the house, which I built on the advice of Jeremiah and under the direction of Anthony McCarthy. Water in the living room, with its slate floor, did no permanent damage. The Persian rugs dried as good as new.

When strikes in Dublin interfered with our supply of electricity Mary and I began considering how important machines had become to us in Dooneen. We could live without an automobile, using bicycles or walking. Our gasoline-powered rotovator could be put in storage, but this would mean reducing the size and efficiency of the garden. A man with a spade can do only so much in the course of a day.

We ground garbage for composting in another gasoline-powered device. Garbage would rot on a compost heap without being ground. The process would be a bit slower.

Could we live without electricity? When it was turned off we lighted candles, which gave the room a warm glow. We read by candlelight and Mary milked by candlelight. Our central heating was electric, but the two fireplaces in the living room and one in the bedroom-study were more or less adequate. We had no hot water.

Our big worry was the deep freeze. In its twenty-five-cubic-foot interior we had a year's supply of food. Should this spoil we would be facing a disaster of considerable proportions. While the power was off we refrained from opening the freezing cabinet for any purpose, to prevent warmer air from entering. We piled newspapers on top of it, to increase the insulation.

We did not know how long the power would be off. We could have taken out some of the food from the deep freeze and after cooking it in the fireplace, put it up in glass jars. Salt might have perserved some of the meat.

We decided to sit tight and hope for the best. Fortunately the electricity came on again before any food in the deep freeze was spoiled.

Meanwhile we cooked in the fireplace at the dining end of the living room, for which Paddy O'Donovan, the Durrus blacksmith, had made a useful grill.

The subject of drains is not a happy one—especially when they go wrong. It seemed unfair that Anthony McCarthy should be asked to repair drains that had been badly installed by another builder, but he was kind about that as he was about everything.

It was only natural that when the great Dooneen water crisis arose we all turned to Anthony. It took us a little time, though, to realize the extent of the crisis we had on our hands.

All of us in Dooneen had been water-proud: other wells and springs might go dry, but not ours. Clear, sparkling spring-water came bubbling down from somewhere on the mountain behind us. There was a storage tank along the road; Jeremiah and Michael McCarthy had installed plastic pipes bringing the water to three houses in Dooneen as well as to barns and even to fields where it was handy to fill water tanks for the cows.

One early spring day I drove by the water tank along the road, giving it a fond glance in passing. Shortly I met a very large machine, in the road, driven by Barry Cronin. I waved and Barry waved and we drove on our separate ways.

Several hours later, when I was back home again, Jeremiah came stomping up with the news that the water supply was "after going muddy." He asked me if I would go up to the storage tank with Jerry and investigate. Jeremiah seemed very disturbed at the idea of Dooneen water dropping below the level of perfection, like an unexpected eclipse of the sun.

As Jerry and I approached the water tank along the road we saw Barry Cronin and his great machine on the side of the mountain. The machine was digging a drainage ditch.

When we investigated the water storage tank we discovered that Barry already had dug there—a deep and wide ditch leading from the spring to the tank itself. The pipe that had carried our drinking water was lying on a pile of earth, not connected with anything at all. Some of the ditch water, how-ever, was trickling into the tank—the source of the muddy water Jeremiah had noted.

We walked up the mountain to Barry Cronin, who turned off the machine so he could hear what we were saying.

"You have just destroyed our water supply!" I shouted.

"I am sorry about that," Barry replied, and he sounded as if he were truly sorry. "I was just doing what I was told to do."

Jerry then explained that the spring was on land owned by his own cousin, Tim O'Donovan. When Jerry's father, Jeremiah, and Michael McCarthy had put in the water catchment and piping system to serve Dooneen they had Tim's oral consent—but no formal, written agreement. Tim had not wanted to sign anything, a common reluctance among Irish farmers and a holdover from the days when contracts with a landlord had always been enforced to the landlord's advantage.

As I was digesting the fact that we in Dooneen were all at the mercy of Tim O'Donovan, Tim himself began walking down the mountain toward where we were standing. When he approached us everyone spoke politely, but finally the subject of water was mentioned.

The destruction of our water supply, it seemed, was related to a rise in the price of milk. Tim wanted to keep more cows. To create more pasture land he conceived the idea of draining the land where our spring was located; a government grant was available for such work. Tim, let it be said, was a good farmer. His plan was a good one.

I could see no real conflict with our water supply. As soon as the drains were dug, I said, Anthony McCarthy could construct a new catchment system at the spring. Pipes taking the water to the storage tank should not interfere with the drainage ditch.

Tim was doubtful. The government drainage inspector might not agree, he said. In my innocence I said I would drive to Bantry and see the inspector. Perhaps he would come out and look over the project and give his verdict on the spot.

This was arranged and we had a famous conference up

there on the side of the mountain, beside the spring. A cold wind blew in from the Atlantic, bringing wisps of rain. We stood under a gray sky—the government inspector, Tim, Jeremiah, Jerry, Michael McCarthy, Anthony and myself. Sometimes the sound of the wind drowned our voices but the trouble went deeper than that.

Anthony outlined the catchment system he proposed to build. Jeremiah, Michael and I agreed to share the cost. The government inspector said he could see no objection.

Tim said nothing. He seemed to be spending a great deal of time looking out over the open ocean, a cloudy vista. In the Irish way no one pressed Tim for a decision. The conference broke up with polite exchanges.

As Jeremiah and Jerry Daly, Michael McCarthy and I walked down the road to Dooneen I pointed out that we had, as yet, no agreement by Tim that we could install a new water system. It was a point no one had missed, but Michael and Jeremiah said it was no real problem.

"Tim won't give us any trouble," said Michael.

Jerry said he would talk to his cousin and see what could be worked out. I suggested that we pay him something for use of the springwater, but Michael and Jeremiah would hear nothing of it.

"I don't think it's money he's after," said Jerry. "Tim isn't like that." Jerry was fond of Tim, as, for that matter, we all were.

Despite all, Jerry was unable to persuade Tim to let us build a water catchment system on his land. I never felt I really understood why.

Meanwhile we began hauling water from the village in plastic containers and milk cans. It was particularly difficult for

Jeremiah, with his herd of cows. We all began thinking of alternative schemes.

The obvious solution was to have a new well bored. This would be expensive. There was no certainty of finding water. There was a shortage of well-boring equipment in the area and the usual experience, we knew, was to wait several months before the services of a well borer could be obtained. Hauling water from the village for several months was not a prospect we welcomed and whether we could arrange to get village water over that period of time was in question.

Jeremiah, understandably, was reluctant to join in the proposal to bore a well. Michael McCarthy said that river water was good enough for his cows; Michael's house and pub had its own water system.

Nevertheless, Mary and I decided to go ahead with the well. I telephoned Paddy Harte in Clonakilty, the nearest well borer, and got his wife on the line. She was both cheerful and encouraging. Her husband, she said, was working with his digger not far from our place and might be willing to put us at the top of the waiting list because he would have to move his machinery only a short distance.

I walked down to the Dalys to report. Jerry said he and his father had been thinking about the well. Jerry, who was taking over management of the farm, said he expected to be farming in Dooneen for many years—and would need a good, dependable supply of water. They agreed to share the expenses of a new well.

When Paddy Harte came to look over the situation, the Dalys, Mary and I joined him in our upper boreen (lane). There, Paddy broke off a forked stick from our privet hedge, held it in his two clenched fists, and the stick turned.

This was the first experience Mary and I had had with dowsing, or divining for water. I had heard of water witches and warlocks. As an educated, rational American I could hardly be expected to believe in such things. Nevertheless I kept quiet while the problem of bringing the machine into our narrow boreen was discussed. Paddy thought there might be a better place.

The Dalys' haggard would give easy access to the machine, he said. Since it was a joint venture it didn't really matter whether the well was on Jeremiah's land or ours. We all went below, Paddy carrying his forked stick from the privet hedge.

There the stick turned again. Unable to restrain myself, I asked if I could try it. Mary later said I looked as if I had seen a leprechaun when the stick also moved in my fists. Then Mary tried it and it moved, and when Jerry tried it the stick twirled around completely. I can only say that this is what happened, not why, or what it meant. Paddy said he would begin drilling for water in the Dalys' haggard the next day.

"What if we don't find water?" I asked.

"There's water there, all right," said Paddy confidently. "If I don't find it, you pay nothing. If the well goes dry I'll come back and make it work." Whatever skepticism about the forked stick I might have obviously was not shared by Paddy Harte.

Even when the drill ground through foot after foot of dry, hard rock, Paddy's confidence was not shaken. Twice, the bit on the drill broke. Paddy drove to Cork for new parts and returned to resume drilling, unperturbed.

When the drill had gone down fifty feet without finding water I began to think I had imagined the forked stick had moved in my fists. Hauling water from Kilcrohane became more arduous than ever. Jeremiah hated going to the pub, to face the inevitable question: "Any water yet?"

Then, at ninety-two feet, the water came.

We all toasted our success with pure well water. The boys at the pub would get their answer at last. Paddy's great well-boring machine lumbered out of the Dalys' haggard.

Although we had water again, we and the Dalys regretted the loss of the old spring. Water from that now bubbled through drainage ditches and a small river to the sea.

Why had Tim O'Donovan refused to let us use it? It was as mysterious as the movement of the forked dowsing stick.

Some Problems Solve Themselves

❧ It isn't really true that if, after wrestling with problems, you simply walk away from them they will all solve themselves. This does happen occasionally, however, especially in Ireland.

The mountains surrounding Dooneen made radio reception notoriously difficult. We tried in vain to make several American radios work properly. Then an electrical goods dealer in Skibbereen, from whom we bought a number of gadgets, threw in a little transistor radio for goodwill. It didn't work very well, either—until we discovered that the one place in the house that it would work was in the windowsill beside our bed. There we could get Irish radio, the BBC or the Voice of America, loud and clear.

We waited a year and a half for a telephone. After it was installed we realized how many tiresome trips we had been forced to make to the public telephone in Kilcrohane to put in calls.

With a radio in working order and a telephone we were

less isolated, whether for good or ill it was difficult to say. The news that came over our little radio more often than not was disquieting; the world outside Dooneen seemed a troubled place. Few telephone calls were of any importance and we often ran upstairs to the bedroom-study, where the telephone had been installed, to no good purpose. For some reason I could never discover, the Bantry telephone people found it necessary to ring us every day to test the line. It showed, I thought, a certain lack of confidence in their own handiwork.

The problem of taking care of the rabbits and ducks, made more difficult by the crude houses I had built for these animals out of the packing cases our household goods were shipped in, did not solve itself. Mary and I drew up careful plans for new housing, and Anthony McCarthy sent over a crew to do the work. A new duck pond filled itself from water runoff. The new rabbit house was built so that we could be under shelter while tending them and so that they could have plenty of fresh air while avoiding a wetting in a gale.

Our problem with the goatling, Joy, nursing the two older milch goats, did solve itself, though. It wasn't that Joy gave up her taste for milk or that the various devices I had tried, to keep her from nursing, really worked. The real cure was named, officially, Finlarig Darwin. We called him Paddy. He was our billy goat, the new leader of the herd.

It is an understatement to say that I was reluctant to get a billy goat. He would have to be housed separately. Someone would have to go to Ballynahinch, in County Down, to get him. He would have to be fed and watered. If allowed to run with the milch goats in the pasture it meant that they would be bred when they were ready—all within the space of a few weeks at most. We could not stagger the breeding so that we always had milk available.

All of these reasons for not having a billy goat involved drains on our limited finances, time and energy. Furthermore, the goat book we trusted most had an ominous section on controlling billy goats. In the end, it said, the goat keeper would have to engage in a wrestling match with the creature—and win. I wasn't sure if I was up to that. What happened if the billy goat won?

The best alternative to owning a billy goat would have been to take each doe to a Saanen buck when she was ready, pay a modest stud fee, and have no further care of the billy. This was not practical because of the remote part of Ireland in which we lived. There were no pedigreed Saanen billy goats in the area. A trip to County Down with each goat as she was ready to be bred not only would be an expensive nuisance, but would be uncertain of success because of the time lag involved.

To my mind, however, there was no real reason why the does could not be bred by any old scrub billy, and such goats were available. The purpose of breeding was not to produce high-milk-yield stock, but to renew the cycle of lactation. The kids produced would still be edible. We could not, in any event, keep the progeny of the best-bred billy as milkers in our own herd, for this, if we kept the same billy, would lead to inbreeding.

Logic was on my side, but tenacity was on Mary's. She wanted a "complete herd" of blooded stock. So we had a new goat house built at the edge of our mountainy pasture to house a billy goat at night and to provide shelter for all of the goats during the daytime. We would continue to bring the milch goats back to their old goat house in the haggard for the night, for convenience of milking and to avoid the possibility of a taint in the milk.

Because our pasture was a part of a scenic area we had to have government permission to build a new goat house there. The planning people insisted it be a low structure, tucked behind a hill. This suited us. Mary's design was both esthetically pleasing and practical.

From the west door of the new goat house one had a breathtaking view of the mouth of Dunmanus Bay, the hills flanking it and the sweep of the open Atlantic beyond. The milch goats gave up the temporary shelters I had built for them without any apparent regrets. When it rained they ran for the new house.

We were ready for the billy goat, or as ready as we would be. The goat farm people in County Down selected him. Mary said she would go up and get him herself.

"He'll be only a little kid," she said. "I'll bring him down on the train; he can sit on my lap."

I pointed out that even the excellent railroad line from Belfast to Dublin to Cork did not include toilet facilities for goats. When the time came I drove the length of the Irish island and brought Paddy home in the van.

The trip was complicated by the fact that Paddy had to be fed frequently on the way. He was, indeed, a small bundle of white fur, a month-old kid. Mary had obtained from America a set of baby nipples and a bottle. I had filled a thermos jug with warm milk at the goat farm.

Unfortunately, Paddy was totally unable to get any milk from the baby nipples. At each feeding I stopped the van and struggled with him—with no result. I tried forcing him to drink the milk directly out of the bottle—still with no result. As he became more and more hungry he made it known by uninterrupted and very loud bleating.

In desperation I picked a likely looking farm, drove into the yard, and presented my predicament to the farmer's wife. She was a woman of compassion and competence.

We let Paddy out of the van and her small children played with him. He stopped bleating. I showed the farm woman the bottle and nipples I was using in an attempt to feed the little goat.

"It's an impossibility you'd be trying," she said. "Whoever heard of a billy goat with a mouth like a baby's? You'll have to be after getting a lamb's teat for the pore creature."

I puzzled over that, but she told me to stop at a chemist's shop in the next town and buy a black rubber nipple of the sort used to feed orphaned lambs. It is, she said, shaped for the mouth of a lamb or a kid and not for a Christian baby.

As I drove off, the bleating in the van resumed, with double force. I did, though, get the lamb's teat; the druggist washed out a bottle to use with it. Then I started to drive out of town with my noisy load, intending to feed Paddy at last in some secluded spot.

There was, however, a traffic jam in town. At the same time Paddy, getting more and more frantic, managed to wedge his foot somewhere in the interior of the van. There was nothing to do but to stop, get out and go around to the back of the van and attend to the goat—traffic jam or no traffic jam.

It was then I noticed that the car immediately behind me was a police car. In most of the countries of the world this situation would have led to one of those protracted and pointless arguments adding up to nothing more, with luck, than a waste of time and tempers. This being Ireland, nothing of the sort happened. The policemen behind me sized up the situation at a glance. They simply pulled their official car around my van and sped off—pretending not to see what was going on at all.

Getting Paddy's leg freed took but a moment. He was not injured. Getting out of town took only a few additional minutes. When Paddy finally was fed all went much better.

When I got Paddy to Dooneen Mary, of course, feel in love with him. She insisted that we bring him right into the house, where he leaped about, happy enough himself, first on the couch, then to a table.

The next day was fine, with a warm sun and clouds billowing white over the mountains. We carried Paddy in our arms, taking turns, as we went to the mountainy pasture. The three milch goats were browsing on flowering heather.

We put Paddy down a hundred yards from the other goats and he just stood there, an uncertain little animal in a strange new place. Then he gave out with one bleat—and Fleur answered. At that, Paddy frolicked over to the herd and joined it. And at the same moment a skylark began his song in the air above us, fitting mood music.

Three months later we were wondering whether the three female goats were not pregnant; a billy goat is that precocious. Some are sexually viable at four months, which was Paddy's age. He was growing so rapidly in size that Jeremiah thought we were feeding him too much and I wondered how I could handle him when he weighed more than I did.

It was important to know if the milch goats were pregnant, for their feeding would have to be adjusted and two months before giving birth they would have to be dried off. A veterinary surgeon looked at the goats and said he simply could not tell whether they were pregnant or not. I doubted it. Mary thought they were and Jeremiah agreed with Mary.

One of our visitors at that time happened to be an American medical doctor, who said there had been developed a quite simple chemical test to find out whether female human beings were pregnant. He said he could see no reason why the test would not work as well for goats.

This suggestion led us on a trail of misunderstanding and frustration. Mary telephoned a woman agricultural instructor in Clonakilty who had visited our farm. She said she knew there was a test sometimes used to discover whether cows were pregnant and gave Mary the name of a laboratory in Cork City which she believed made such tests. Mary telephoned the laboratory.

That conversation was somewhat complicated by the fact that the girl answering the phone in the Cork laboratory thought that Mary wanted to know whether she was herself pregnant. The idea of a pregnant goat apparently was too outlandish to merit serious consideration.

The laboratory girl suggested that Mary call the Irish Department of Agriculture in Dublin. Mary did that. A man answered, confidently aware that a female goat might or might not be pregnant. Tests to determine this fact could be performed by the department, he assured Mary. The thing to do was to obtain samples of the urine of the goats in question and send them along in bottles, plainly marked.

Following three female goats around a rocky mountain pasture while carrying sterile vessels in which to catch their urine added nothing to my dignity, but it had to be done, it seemed. The urine, captured, bottled and labeled, was sent off to Dublin by post. I did not think it necessary to describe the contents of the package, at the post office.

There was some delay before we heard from the Department of Agriculture. Finally the verdict came, on impressive stationery.

"I regret we cannot assist you," wrote the Department of Agriculture official. "Pregnancy diagnosis by this method only applies to horses and donkeys among the domestic animals."

We were left to conjecture for ourselves as to the results of Paddy's youthful fumbling. The euphemism in our parish for a female animal coming into heat is to say that she has "gone to dairy." When the three female goats began wagging their tails and showing a new interest in Paddy it seemed reasonably clear that they weren't yet pregnant. It was a situation Paddy by then was able to handle.

Paddy was developing into a giant of a goat. He certainly came to weigh well over 200 pounds and was as tall as a pony. His interest did not stop with our three females. When a little female goat which ran with Michael McCarthy's cows went to dairy, Paddy threatened to go through the fence after her.

We had no objection to this conquest but only feared for our fence. I tried to catch the female goat to bring her inside the pasture but she was very shy of human beings, though not of Paddy. As soon as I stopped chasing her she would return to the fence and call to Paddy.

To save the fence I decided to shut up Paddy in the goat house. This meant dragging him, kicking and bellowing, more than a hundred yards across the mountain. Fortunately, Paddy had not quite reached his full size at that point, but he was heavy enough.

Meanwhile, our own three female goats became more and more obviously pregnant. Gradually we ceased milking them and as they dried up, Joy's source of milk vanished. She seemed not to miss it. Of their matings with Paddy, Fleur gave birth to three male kids and Katrina and Joy to one female each.

Mary's judgment, in letting Joy nurse well into adulthood, was justified by experience. Joy's ability to convert green foliage into milk was not hampered; she became the best milker in the herd. She did not go back to nursing after kidding.

We sold the female kids as milkers, for a good price, and had the male goats butchered and put the meat in the deep freeze. Mary wept a bit at these events but accepted them as inevitable.

Love, the Sea and the Mountains

When Mary and I met Jeremiah on the road he often asked the question: "And how are all your care?" It was a question that embraced all of our animals, our garden, buildings and land as well as ourselves.

When friends came to stay with us we found it natural to introduce them to Jeremiah. No matter how well we had known them in another setting we knew them better after watching their reactions to Jeremiah, and his reaction to them. If they had his approval, Jeremiah would say: "Welcome to the land!"

Jeremiah's authority in Dooneen was not diminished when he turned the farm over to his son Jerry. That was a part of the natural progression of events, like Jerry's marriage to Elizabeth Lehane. Jeremiah's authority had been earned by being himself for sixty-odd years. It would continue until he died.

Mary and I had many young friends in the parish, but the new generation, for us, meant especially Elizabeth Lehane and her elder sister, Mary Lehane. The Lehanes lived several miles away from Dooneen, up the mountain east of the village, but our relationship with them had begun the first year we had used our Irish home as a vacation place.

While we were staying in Dooneen a message arrived from my daughter, Ann, by then Mrs. Frank Davidoff of Lexington, Massachusetts. Ann cabled that she desperately needed someone to come and stay with them for a year—and could we find a nice Irish girl? Ann Davidoff, in addition to being the mother of three children, was director of a nursery school. She needed a "mother's helper."

We consulted our friends and neighbors. The girl most often suggested was Mary Lehane. Although only sixteen years old, she had left school and was working in a Bantry pub. She was not a "barmaid," as the term is understood in America; Mary was a pretty young girl, shy, but obviously capable and willing to take responsibility.

As a part of the arrangement, Mary and I insisted that Mary Lehane return to Ireland after a year in America. It was, I think, a good year for Mary Lehane. It also was a great change from the life she had known in Kilcrohane and Bantry. She returned with a new respect for the value of education, for one thing.

We enlisted the help of Father Walsh and of Father Keating in getting her enrolled in St. Mary's convent school in Dunmanway. Mary Lehane was a good student and the nuns took a great liking to her. While in Dunmanway she decided she wanted to become a trained nurse. Her academic preparation for nurse's training in Ireland was not adequate, but English standards were somewhat more relaxed. The nuns arranged for Mary to enter a convent nursing school in England. Dunmanway is about halfway to Cork City. Mary and I visited the convent several times while Mary Lehane was there; it was a lovely spot. Mary Lehane was full of plans for the future.

Then, at the last minute, she changed her mind. Instead of going to England to have nurse's training, she returned to North America. It was a blow to us and also to the good nuns who had taken such an interest in their excellent pupil. Perhaps Mary also felt that her early academic training was not sufficient for the nursing school, but there was another reason for her decision.

While working in Bantry she had met a young man named Neeley Keohane. Neeley had followed Mary Lehane to America. Later, he got a job in Canada and was still there. When she left the convent, Mary also went to Canada.

We had, it seemed, been instrumental in losing for Ireland not one young person, but two. Also, Mary and I could not help worrying about Mary Lehane in North America; she was still very young. We did not know Neeley Keohane.

Mary and Elizabeth were the daughters of Con Lehane, the winner of the famous Kilcrohane carnival horse race, and of Betty, his wife—a handsome, strong woman who sometimes plowed ground by herself, handling horse and plow, as they said, "like any man." We often met Con and Betty in Kilcrohane after Mass, and also Betty's mother, Mrs. O'Sullivan. None of them, however, seemed to know what the future held in store for Mary Lehane.

Shortly after we moved permanently to Dooneen the Mary Lehane story began to unravel. Mary's parents told us that she was coming home for a visit. We wanted to see her of course, but what about this Neeley Keohane? No one seemed to know.

But when Mary Lehane arrived in Kilcrohane, Neeley was with her. They spent an evening with us in Dooneen and gave us the news: they had come home, they said, to be married at the Star of the Sea.

We got out our best glasses and china. It was a celebration. My Mary immediately wanted to know if she might bake the wedding cake and Mary Lehane said she would be delighted by that.

We were happy, not only because we shared Mary Lehane's obvious happiness, but also because of the sort of a young man Neeley Keohane was. He was attractive, friendly and intelligent—and had about him a feeling of steady capability. He seemed to be a young man who could make his way under any circumstances, and would take good care of Mary Lehane. His name, Neeley, was short for Cornelius, as Con, as Mary's father was called, was another shortened form of the same name.

The only thing we didn't like was that Neeley said they must return to Canada after the wedding. He said his family owned a farm near Bantry, not now being used much. By working in Canada he hoped to earn enough to fix up the farm, where he and Mary might one day come to live.

In the days that followed, our kitchen was a busy place. An Irish wedding cake, I discovered, is no simple matter. It is a gigantic, three-tiered affair, filled with fruit and nuts, elaborately frosted and decorated. It had to be big enough to feed nearly a hundred wedding guests, with enough left over so that pieces could be mailed to well-wishers in the United States, Canada and England.

Obtaining the proper ingredients for the cake took a bit of doing. Mary sent to America for the decorations. Among other things, the cake with all those ingredients must be made carefully. Mary worked with her usual care and patience. When the cake was finished we lived in terror for fear a wayward mouse would elect to become the first of the wedding guests to taste it.

It was a happy day when Neeley and Mary stood up at the Star of the Sea and took the marriage vows. Mary's sister, Elizabeth, was the bridesmaid. The bells rang and rice was thrown. It was a fortunate ending to a perilous journey for Mary Lehane, I couldn't help thinking. She looked radiant in a white satin dress she had brought with her from America. Elizabeth was a beautiful bridesmaid as well—as Jerry Daly did not fail to notice.

After the church ceremony, conducted by the parish priest, Father McSwiney, and the curate, Father Boland, the wedding guests piled in automobiles to drive to Skibbereen, thirty miles away. There, in the West Cork Hotel, a midday dinner was waiting, complete with champagne. Father Boland was master of ceremonies and many songs were sung. Mary Keohane cut her wedding cake.

Then began the long hours of dancing, with both older dances and modern styles popular. Old and young whirled around the dance floor to the music of a hired band. Father Boland was the star of the dance floor. Mary Lehane's grandmother danced with the best of them.

From time to time the dancing was interrupted by volunteers who went to the platform to sing, Irish songs, old and new. Margaret Tobin, sister of Jim Tobin, whose goats had wandered into the Star of the Sea church, sang sweetly. There was a fine song by Carmel, the sister of Anthony McCarthy, the builder who had helped us so many times in making our home in Dooneen more livable and had constructed houses for our animals.

The best of all the singing, Mary and I thought, was by Mary Lehane's own mother, Betty. She did not go to the platform, or use the microphone. Instead, from her chair at the edge of the dance floor she sang in a surprisingly beautiful voice the ballad of "My Little Daughter, Nell," sad enough to bring tears to your eyes, but charming. It was followed by crashing applause by Betty's friends and neighbors, proud to know the mother of the bride who could sing a song or plow a field as the occasion demanded.

Neeley's parents were there, of course, and Mary and I met them for the first time. They were quiet and decent people. Neeley's mother agreed that it would be a wonderful thing if the newlyweds, instead of returning to Canada, could somehow stay in Ireland.

"But Neeley is set on going," his mother said. "He must do what he thinks best."

Neeley's old shop-mates at the garage in Bantry, where he had worked before going to Canada, had come out in force. John Barry, the garage owner—from whom we had bought our little Ford van—also came to the wedding.

"Neeley is as good a boy as you'll find," he said. "I wish we had him back."

The talking was as important as the dancing. Friends and relations of Mary and Neeley had become our own friends and neighbors since we had moved to Muintirvara Parish. There was Frances Tobin, the schoolteacher who had brought her class to Dooneen to see the goats, and Paddy Spillane, one of the few farmers in the parish who grew oats and who often let us have some.

Jeremiah and I stood to one side most of the time, smoking our pipes and talking to each other and to the other guests who came along. It was a different setting from the places we usually met—on the lane to the pasture, in his haggard or ours or in the shelter of the Daly barn with its wide open doors and odors of hay and of cows. The talk, though, was much the same—about people, animals and crops.

The pounding of the music of the dance band went on and on. Smoke from cigars, cigarettes and pipes filled the ballroom.

The ceremony at the Star of the Sea had been in the morning. It was well past dark before Mary Lehane tossed her bridal bouquet and she and Neeley drove away to begin their honeymoon. First, though, Neeley had to untie the tin cans which had been fastened to the rear of his automobile; an Irish wedding would not have been complete without that touch.

After the bride and bridegroom left, the guests began to drift away. A few showed the effects of the party and Mary and I were a bit worried about the drivers on those narrow and dark roads. There were, however, no serious incidents.

Back at our own fireside, Mary and I went over the day again, enjoying it. How soon, we wondered, would there be another such celebration—for the marriage of Jerry Daly and Elizabeth Lehane? That would, indeed, be an important event for all of us living in Dooneen. We also speculated on the future of Mary Lehane—as Mrs. Neeley Keohane.

We were to learn more about that very soon, and the news was good. When Neeley and Mary returned from their honeymoon they announced that they had decided, after all, not to go back to Canada. Neeley found a job on a dredge boat working in the Dingle harbor in Kerry. It was a job that paid enough so that they could put something aside to fix up the old farm outside Bantry. Their future would be in Ireland, as we had hoped.

A year after Neeley and Mary were married, Jerry and Elizabeth took the vows at the Star of the Sea. They were a handsome couple.

Since we had first met Jerry Daly, my Mary had been urging him to get married, suggesting first one girl in the parish and then another. Jerry only smiled and kept his own counsel. We were both happy when we learned that he had chosen Mary Lehane's younger sister, a tall and quite beautiful girl. Elizabeth was only eighteen years old when they were married.

Neeley and Mary Keohane were in the church for the marriage of Jerry and Elizabeth. In her arms, Mary Keohane held their firstborn, also named Cornelius. During the marriage Mass the sound of little Cornelius gurgling and crying made a fitting obbligato.

It was a warm day, though in February, and the church doors were open. From outside the church came the sounds of a rooster crowing, a blackbird singing and the clip-clop of a horse, pulling a cartload of milk to the creamery.

As on the previous occasion, we all drove to Skibbereen after the ceremony for a great dinner and for dancing afterwards. Again, the wedding cake was my Mary's handiwork. Once more a happy couple drove off on their honeymoon.

Some neighbors had suggested that Elizabeth and her mother-in-law, Kathleen Daly, would be bound to clash, both being women of strong characters. They were wrong. Elizabeth, despite her youth, proved to be a thoughtful and cooperative housewife, a strong helper with the chores and a good neighbor.

Perhaps a new generation in Dooneen might have made Mary and me feel older, but in fact it did not. Marriage, birth, growth and death were all a part of living; our own lives were meshed with it all. It was a fine thing to see Jerry and Elizabeth working together across the way. It somehow made Mary and me, also working together, seem younger ourselves.

Life in many forms was in constant motion around us. Mating and birth were at the heart of the rhythm, in the ocean itself as well as on land.

We made a memorable trip to Carbery Island to watch the seals there. As we lay in the grass on the heights above the shore on the island the seals appeared, one by one, diving for fish in the surf. Then we noticed that the seals also were watching us. They lined up, facing the shore, their big eyes bulging. A few minutes later they brought the baby seals over to see us, as well; the people-watching seals gave short, staccato barks, a comment.

Just out from Carbery Island was a small, bare rock. As the tide receded the exposed surface of the rock enlarged. Suddenly a big old seal hoisted himself onto the rock, swayed his head from side to side and began making a strange noise. It was not a bark, this time, but a long, drawn-out wail.

Soon the first seal was joined by another, which also began to sing. Then a third seal joined them on the rock, and a fourth, and, finally, a fifth. The five seals weaved back and forth, their snouts in the air, each singing a song of its own. It was a lusty chorus, no doubt beautiful to the ears of a seal and impressive enough to ourselves. We could only believe that the first seal had been a bull and that the other four were members of his harem. The mating season had begun.

As we left the island there was a fog hanging over Dunmanus Bay. Through it, from our boat, we could see the seals but dimly, though their singing still was strong. It would have been easy enough to imagine that there were mermaids and other strange creatures out there on the rock.

There was a full moon shining over the bay that night. When Job and I went to the mountainy pasture to care for the goats we listened in the stillness. From far out on the bay the sound of the singing seals could still be heard, a cry of love and mystery in the night.

Then one day when I was driving back from Bantry over the Goats' Path road I was witness to an event that somehow, for me, united our own, tame farming kind of life in Dooneen with a wilder sort of life in the mountains around us. Since we had given away the first two billy goats born in Dooneen, and later heard that one of them had been allowed to escape to the mountain, I had been worrying vaguely about the mountain goats. One would catch a glimpse of two or three of them, in the distance. Mary and I both made a habit of looking for them whenever we took the Goats' Path road over Seefinn.

In dry weather, farmers often burned the mountain, thinking this might renew the common pasturage where they kept their sheep. We disliked this practice for many reasons, including what it might do to the wild goats there.

It was after just such a mountain fire that I drove over the Goats' Path road one day and saw, for the first time, the entire wild goat herd. They had been driven from their remote retreat by the fire. There they were, some of them even on the road in front of the van. I stopped the van, feeling myself to be an alien invader.

There were, in all, at least fifteen wild goats in the herd, perhaps more, including a number of kids beside their mothers. But it was the herd leader that caught my attention—a great white buck with magnificent horns and a flowing beard. He gave me one fierce look before he wheeled and led the entire herd galloping up the side of the mountain.

From that moment I had no doubt at all about the identity of the great white buck. He was the son of our own senior milch goat, Fleur—a pure-bred Saanen, wild and free.

Watching him go up the mountain I couldn't help remembering those two little male kids we had helped out of their mother's womb, had toweled dry and cared for. How different it must be for him now, searching for heather and gorse to crop on the burned-over mountain, seeking water in whatever spring might still be running in so dry a season. I caught my breath in sad excitement.

Then the great white buck, mounting a high rock above me, stopped for a moment and raised his head, before rushing on. It was a posture of pride and freedom. As I watched, one of the little kids in the herd climbed to the rock beside him, before they both turned away and vanished, leaping. And I was glad.

Appendix

≫ If you are thinking of retiring to a farm in Ireland, here are a few things to bear in mind, based on the experience of the author and his wife.

Prices have increased in Ireland over the last few years. We did it for less, but today you should plan to spend at least $25,000 for a modest house and to pay someone for remodeling it. This figure would include the cost of up to three acres of land, but the cost of animals and farm machinery would be in addition.

If you expect to be subsistence farmers, as we are, you will need an income from other sources of $250 a month, at a minimum.

Once you have a comfortable house and have managed to establish an operation that will provide most of your own food you can live very well indeed on this modest income. By living well I mean that you will have the essentials; your food will be much better than if purchased at a city grocery and your housing and surroundings will be better in every respect than you can obtain in a city at any price. I assume you are prepared to give up a lot of wild luxuries with which city people try to compensate themselves for the basically barren sort of life a city provides. We found this no loss.

In general it is preferable to buy an old farmhouse and remodel it, rather than build a new house. Traditional stone farmhouses are designed for the climate and land of rural Ireland. Their sites usually are well chosen and the stone hedges which often surround them are invaluable. On the coast of West Cork, protection from gales is at least as important as a view of the sea. In the city, you may dream of living at the edge of a cliff overlooking the open Atlantic. You will live to regret it if you allow yourself to get carried away by such a vision.

We think a fireplace is essential; our small house has three. On the other hand, central heating is imperative—especially for Americans. Fireplaces alone do not keep a house from being cold and damp in some seasons.

Try to be on hand while your house is being remodeled. The job needs watching in Ireland as elsewhere. Consult a good Irish solicitor before you buy and remodel a place; he can save you later headaches.

You can learn to operate a small farm even if you know nothing about farming now. There are many books on the subject. Irish and American Department of Agriculture bulletins and pamphlets are helpful. Ireland has an Agricultural Instructor service that can be consulted on the spot.

It takes long hours of hard work, however. It is not easy to hire someone to help you. Before you decide to be a farmer be sure you have the necessary physical stamina.

Remember, also, that working hard, in some isolation and in the face of new and often difficult problems, puts a strain on any marriage. It might be well to consider whether yours can stand such a strain.

In the end, of course, it all depends on what you want. Obviously, if you prefer concrete sidewalks and crowds, retirement to rural Ireland doesn't make sense. If your idea of fun is to go shopping, coming to West Cork to farm doesn't make much sense, either. New York's Fifth Avenue is a long way off.

Furthermore, if you are keeping animals on a farm you must pretty well give up the idea of travel altogether. We often are asked when we take our holidays. The answer is: never. Animals require constant care, 365 days a year.

I suppose you have to be built in a certain way to retire to rural Ireland and be happy. Face yourself honestly. It really doesn't make much difference whether your ancestors came from Ireland or not. Sentimental Irish songs are a poor basis for trying to build a new life on an Irish farm.

It is necessary, I think, to visit Ireland as a tourist before making up your mind about retiring to an Irish farm. Stay in bed-and-breakfast places in rural areas: they are the best buys, anyway. Observe thoughtfully. Talk to people of many different sorts. Read books about Ireland. Not all areas of Ireland are the same.

West Cork, which is the part of rural Ireland we know best, is a place of open spaces, mountains and the sea. It is a place where one can live in happy proximity to nature, which here is in a benign mood for the most part—there are no snakes and no poison ivy. Winters are wet but not cold. Summers are cool and pleasant. It is a quiet place, not yet excessively cluttered with human beings and their artifacts. The people are friendly if you meet them halfway.

Differences between Ireland and wherever you were born and reared can be interesting—or irritating. It depends on you.

If you could manage to do it, as a trial run, you might spend a day working outdoors somewhere along the coast of Ireland in winter, with a wet gale blowing. If, at the end of such a day, you can still believe that retirement to an Irish farm is the best life you can think of, it probably is the life for you, as it is for us.